The Little White Book of New Spirit Astrology

Johan Adkins

Bon Nuit Publishing, Cheyenne, WY 82009

Dedicated to
Spirit.
Thanks for all the good stuff

All rights reserved. The card, graphic digital art and content of this book and subsequent books may not be reproduced or duplicated in any way, in any form whatsoever without permission of the publisher.
© 2015 Bon Nuit Publishing
http://www.newspiritastrology.com/index.html

The Little White Book of New Spirit Astrology
Body, Mind and Spirit/Astrology/General

ISBN 978-0-9827589-8-4
ISBN 10 DIGIT 0-982758987
Library of Congress #1-2114760721

Bon Nuit Publishing
7410 Cattlemans Drive
Cheyenne, WY 82009

USA
First Printing 2015

The Little White Book of New Spirit Astrology by Johan Adkins

Table of Contents
Preface
The New Spirit Astrology System is Something New Altogether:
   Explanation of the Difference between the New Spirit
   Astrology System and Traditional Astrology.
Quick Guide to How to Work with the New Spirit Astrology System
Easy Step-by-Step Method of Reading the New Spirit Astrology Cards
Easy Graph Chart - Planet and House Cross-Reference Chart With Page Number Reference
   Sample of how to use the Chart: Necessary tool to find the
   full chart by finding the House where Sun 1 is located.
   Actual Charts

Full Charts (all twelve combinations)

Basis	Chart 1
Value	Chart 2
Conscious Mind	Chart 3
Subconscious Mind	Chart 4
Love Aspect	Chart 5
Physical Aspect	Chart 6
Emotional Aspect	Chart 7
Generation	Chart 8
Regeneration	Chart 9
Universal Lifeforce	Chart 10
Universal Loveforce	Chart 11
Karma	Chart 12

Planets in the Houses
The Planets are always in this order: Sun 1, Moon 1, Earth/Venus 1, Mars, Neptune, Saturn, Uranus, Minerva, Sun 2, Moon 2, Earth/Venus 2, and Mercury.

Sun 1 in the 1st	House (Chart 1)
Sun 1 in the 2nd	House (Chart 2)
Sun 1 in the 3rd	House (Chart 3)
Sun 1 in the 4th	House (Chart 4)
Sun 1 in the 5th	House (Chart 5)
Sun 1 in the 6th	House (Chart 6)
Sun 1 in the 7th	House (Chart 7)
Sun 1 in the 8th	House (Chart 8)

Sun 1 in the 9th	House (Chart 9)
Sun 1 in the 10th	House (Chart 10)
Sun 1 in the 11th	House (Chart 11)
Sun 1 in the 12th	House (Chart 12)
Moon 1 in the 1st	House (Chart 12)
Moon 1 in the 2nd	House (Chart 1)
Moon 1 in the 3rd	House (Chart 2)
Moon 1 in the 4th	House (Chart 3)
Moon 1 in the 5th	House (Chart 4)
Moon 1 in the 6th	House (Chart 5)
Moon 1 in the 7th	House (Chart 6)
Moon 1 in the 8th	House (Chart 7)
Moon 1 in the 9th	House (Chart 8)
Moon 1 in the 10th	House (Chart 9)
Moon 1 in the 11th	House (Chart 10)
Moon 1 in the 12th	House (Chart 11)
Earth/Venus 1 in the 1st	House (Chart 11)
Earth/Venus 1 in the 2nd	House (Chart 12)
Earth/Venus 1 in the 3rd	House (Chart 1)
Earth/Venus 1 in the 4th	House (Chart 2)
Earth/Venus 1 in the 5th	House (Chart 3)
Earth/Venus 1 in the 6th	House (Chart 4)
Earth/Venus 1 in the 7th	House (Chart 5)
Earth/Venus 1 in the 8th	House (Chart 6)
Earth/Venus 1 in the 9th	House (Chart 7)
Earth/Venus 1 in the 10th	House (Chart 8)
Earth/Venus 1 in the 11th	House (Chart 9)
Earth/Venus 1 in the 12th	House (Chart 10)
Mars in the 1st	House (Chart 10)
Mars in the 2nd	House (Chart 11)
Mars in the 3rd	House (Chart 12)
Mars in the 4th	House (Chart 1)
Mars in the 5th	House (Chart 2)
Mars in the 6th	House (Chart 3)
Mars in the 7th	House (Chart 4)
Mars in the 8th	House (Chart 5)
Mars in the 9th	House (Chart 6)
Mars in the 10th	House (Chart 7)
Mars in the 11th	House (Chart 8)
Mars in the 12th	House (Chart 9)

Neptune in the 1st	House	(Chart 9)
Neptune in the 2nd	House	(Chart 10)
Neptune in the 3rd	House	(Chart 11)
Neptune in the 4th	House	(Chart 12)
Neptune in the 5th	House	(Chart 1)
Neptune in the 6th	House	(Chart 2)
Neptune in the 7th	House	(Chart 3)
Neptune in the 8th	House	(Chart 4)
Neptune in the 9th	House	(Chart 5)
Neptune in the 10th	House	(Chart 6)
Neptune in the 11th	House	(Chart 7)
Neptune in the 12th	House	(Chart 8)
Saturn in the 1st	House	(Chart 8)
Saturn in the 2nd	House	(Chart 9)
Saturn in the 3rd	House	(Chart 10)
Saturn in the 4th	House	(Chart 11)
Saturn in the 5th	House	(Chart 12)
Saturn in the 6th	House	(Chart 1)
Saturn in the 7th	House	(Chart 2)
Saturn in the 8th	House	(Chart 3)
Saturn in the 9th	House	(Chart 4)
Saturn in the 10th	House	(Chart 5)
Saturn in the 11th	House	(Chart 6)
Saturn in the 12th	House	(Chart 7)
Uranus in the 1st	House	(Chart 7)
Uranus in the 2nd	House	(Chart 8)
Uranus in the 3rd	House	(Chart 9)
Uranus in the 4th	House	(Chart 10)
Uranus in the 5th	House	(Chart 11)
Uranus in the 6th	House	(Chart 12)
Uranus in the 7th	House	(Chart 1)
Uranus in the 8th	House	(Chart 2)
Uranus in the 9th	House	(Chart 3)
Uranus in the 10th	House	(Chart 4)
Uranus in the 11th	House	(Chart 5)
Uranus in the 12th	House	(Chart 6)
Minerva in the 1st	House	(Chart 6)
Minerva in the 2nd	House	(Chart 7)
Minerva in the 3rd	House	(Chart 8)
Minerva in the 4th	House	(Chart 9)

Minerva in the 5th	House (Chart 10)
Minerva in the 6th	House (Chart 11)
Minerva in the 7th	House (Chart 12)
Minerva in the 8th	House (Chart 1)
Minerva in the 9th	House (Chart 2)
Minerva in the 10th	House (Chart 3)
Minerva in the 11th	House (Chart 4)
Minerva in the 12th	House (Chart 5)
Sun 2 in the 1st	House (Chart 5)
Sun 2 in the 2nd	House (Chart 6)
Sun 2 in the 3rd	House (Chart 7)
Sun 2 in the 4th	House (Chart 8)
Sun 2 in the 5th	House (Chart 9)
Sun 2 in the 6th	House (Chart 10)
Sun 2 in the 7th	House (Chart 11)
Sun 2 in the 8th	House (Chart 12)
Sun 2 in the 9th	House (Chart 1)
Sun 2 in the 10th	House (Chart 2)
Sun 2 in the 11th	House (Chart 3)
Sun 2 in the 12th	House (Chart 4)
Moon 2 in the 1st	House (Chart 4)
Moon 2 in the 2nd	House (Chart 5)
Moon 2 in the 3rd	House (Chart 6)
Moon 2 in the 4th	House (Chart 7)
Moon 2 in the 5th	House (Chart 8)
Moon 2 in the 6th	House (Chart 9)
Moon 2 in the 7th	House (Chart 10)
Moon 2 in the 8th	House (Chart 11)
Moon 2 in the 9th	House (Chart 12)
Moon 2 in the 10th	House (Chart 1)
Moon 2 in the 11th	House (Chart 2)
Moon 2 in the 12th	House (Chart 3)
Earth/Venus 2 in the 1st	House (Chart 3)
Earth/Venus 2 in the 2nd	House (Chart 4)
Earth/Venus 2 in the 3rd	House (Chart 5)
Earth/Venus 2 in the 4th	House (Chart 6)
Earth/Venus 2 in the 5th	House (Chart 7)
Earth/Venus 2 in the 6th	House (Chart 8)
Earth/Venus 2 in the 7th	House (Chart 9)
Earth/Venus 2 in the 8th	House (Chart 10)

Earth/Venus 2 in the 9th   House (Chart 11)
Earth/Venus 2 in the 10th   House (Chart 12)
Earth/Venus 2 in the 11th   House (Chart 1)
Earth/Venus 2 in the 12th   House (Chart 2)
Mercury in the 1st   House (Chart 2)
Mercury in the 2nd   House (Chart 3)
Mercury in the 3rd   House (Chart 4)
Mercury in the 4th   House (Chart 5)
Mercury in the 5th   House (Chart 6)
Mercury in the 6th   House (Chart 7)
Mercury in the 7th   House (Chart 8)
Mercury in the 8th   House (Chart 9)
Mercury in the 9th   House (Chart 10)
Mercury in the 10th   House (Chart 11)
Mercury in the 11th   House (Chart 12)
Mercury in the 12th   House (Chart 1)

Quick Planetary Guide
    Sun 1
    Moon 1
    Earth/Venus 1
    Mars
    Neptune
    Saturn
    Uranus
    Minerva
    Sun 2
    Moon 2
    Earth/Venus 2
    Mercury

Quick House Guide
    House 1- House of Basis
    House 2- House of Values
    House 3- House of Conscious Mind
    House 4- House of Subconscious Mind
    House 5- House of Love Aspect
    House 6- House of Physical Aspect
    House 7- House of Emotional Aspect
    House 8- House of Generation
    House 9- House of Regeneration

House 10- House of Universal Lifeforce
House 11- House of Universal Loveforce
House 12- House of Karma

Quick Elemental Guide
Fire
Air-Ether
Water
Earth
Wood
Metal

Emphasis Cards
Physical
Emotional
Spiritual

Divinity Cards (all on the same page)

Card 1	Yes	
Card 2	No	
Card 3	I don't know or I can't answer	
Card 4	Regroup the cards, cleanse, and try later	
Card 5	It is not to your highest good to answer at this time	
Card 6	Rephrase your question and focus	

Blank Cards
Handy Reference Guide, Graphs and Charts
Condensed Sort of aspects by House
Glossary and Something Else; Johan's Story
Closing Comments by Johan Adkins
About the Author
Books and Contact Sources Johan Adkins, Author
Review of *Prismland* and *Earth 1* by *Writer's Digest Magazine*
Excerpt from *Earth 1* by Johan Adkins

Preface

This book is written as a companion to *New Spirit Astrology Cards,* an astrology deck authored by Johan Adkins. Each deck is numbered and includes a signed Certificate of Authenticity.

The New Spirit Astrology deck can be purchased through the website http://www.newspiritastrology.com/index.html

The cards are designed to help guide your soul's progress through twelve Houses to reach spiritual oneness at the end of your many lives. From just two cards, a Planetary Card and a House Card, a full reading in twelve different aspects or areas of your life can help you reach that goal.

The New Spirit Astrology deck has a total of 45 cards: 12 Planetary Cards, 12 House Cards, 6 Elemental Cards, 3 Emphasis Cards, 6 Divinity Cards, and 6 Blank Cards. Blank Cards can be used as section dividers or can be assigned their own Divinity value by the deck owner.

All of the cards are beautifully designed by the author, Johan Adkins and Oil and Graphic Artist, Gloria Jean of Colorado.

Please store the deck in numeric order with the Blank Cards in between sections, and kept in a designated bag or wooden box. Stones and crystals or non-iodized sea salt can keep the deck charged and protected.

The New Spirit Astrology System is something new altogether

In traditional astrology, the position of the planets in relation to the Sun and to each other was the basis for centuries of differing opinions about what these attributes signified. The exacting mathematical calculations involved were given many arbitrary meanings and and differed greatly from culture to culture and over time.

In the New Spirit Astrology System, life is simplified.

> This system is based around the precept that the planets themselves are living entities that exchange energy with each other, as need demands in order to keep our solar system intact. The Sun is at the center and is the Godhead to all others. The four Planets that have the most to do with human transformation are: the Sun; the Moon; Earth; and Venus. Mars, Neptune, Saturn, Uranus, Minerva and Mercury Planetary energies also contribute as teachers or secondary teachers.

The planets have male, female, and sometimes androgynous attributes. Ultimately, there is a delicate balance in our Universe of two types of energies which ebb and flow through the planets' poles and across our solar system. This balance is comprised of dual energies called Loveforce and Lifeforce, the true yin and yang. Lifeforce can be described roughly as "head-oriented" and Loveforce as "heart-oriented." Each planet was born in a certain order to the Sun, with a certain recipe of Loveforce and Lifeforce energy, establishing each one in a unique place in the hierarchy of power. Jupiter and Pluto do not show up in the cards since the energy extended from them and to them is negligible in our human transformational process.

Traditional Western astrology assigned attributes to Houses. In the New Spirit Astrology System, the attributes of these Houses help us understand the vagaries of our day-to-day lives; what we need to work on; and where we are in our transformational journey. They can also help us comprehend the journeys of our fellow spiritual travelers as well.

The Divinity Cards are included as a built-in check and balance system to help give readers a means by which to speak with Spirit directly in the safe environment of this system of cards. The Emphasis Cards help fine tune the reading to determine whether it is a Physical, Emotional or Spiritual reading. Blank Cards help simplify the reading if a particular aspect doesn't enter into the picture, or they serve as a place-marker to determine whether the cards to be read as Level 1 or Level 2.

I know you're going to love the New Spirit Astrology System!

Johan Adkins

How to Work With the New Spirit Astrology System

(Quick Method)

A wise person once said that a good "reader" could read blank cards. The cards help you access your higher-self or that part of yourself which already intuits the answers.

It is recommended by the author, of course, that you purchase *The New Spirit Astrology* Cards by Johan Adkins. You can create your own cards if you wish. Use the cards when your body is clean and clear. Alcohol or drug usage and/or working in an unclean area will give you a false reading. Try bathing and fasting for the optimal effect and work when you are not distracted by interruptions. The work area also needs to be cleansed and prepared. Soothing music, plants, and flowers increase the vibration of the reading. If you do make your own cards, please use the protective symbol of the fleur de lys (shape of the iris flower) on the backs of your cards.

The book itself can be used in place of cards. Focus, pose the question in your mind clearly, state it three times, silently or aloud, and then open the book. The place your eyes light upon should give you insight; if not, the answer is probably somewhere on the page, or you can run your fingers over the top right edge of the book and insert a fingernail and open it from there.

You can shuffle all the cards together and use the New Spirit Astrology Cards any way you want. As long as you are clean, the area is clean, the cards are cleansed, you focus, and you state a positive proper request clearly three times, you can't do anything wrong. Just refer to the Table of Contents to find the charts which direct you to the meanings of what you have drawn.

If you want ultra-simplicity, just think of your question and visually choose your cards.

EASY STEP-BY-STEP METHOD

The step-by-step method of reading is optional, but it was developed in order to give you the most accurate reading possible.

HOW TO DO A SIMPLE READING

For the very best results, it is highly recommended that you are clean, the area is clean, the cards are cleansed, and that you relax, focus and state your question in the form of the *three-fold request* or repeat; "I ask this question in the perfect way, the perfect number of times." Many people resist any ritual of this nature; however, if you do not state your request in threes, you may not get an accurate reading. Think of it this way: the first statement rings a doorbell; with the second statement, Spirit answers the door; and with the third statement, Spirit listens to what you have to say.

Separate your deck into 6 categories: Planetary Cards 1-12, House Cards 1-12, Elemental Cards 1-6, Emphasis Cards 1-3, Divinity Cards 1-6, Blank Cards 1-6.

Alternative One:

Draw a Planetary Card: This card will give you an overview of the situation.

Draw a House Card: This will pinpoint the area affected.

Draw an Elemental Card: This will show you the challenges you must overcome and the lessons you must learn.

Draw an Emphasis Card: These cards pinpoint the area to focus on and show whether the reading is Physical, Emotional, or Spiritual. All three apply, but one area may be predominant for the reading.

The Divinity Cards: These cards are included as a built-in check and balance system providing a means by which you may speak with Spirit directly in the safe environment of The New Spirit Astrology System. They can be worked with alone or not incorporated at all.

Alternative Two: Preparation for Full or Comprehensive Chart

Draw a Planetary Card: This card will give you an overview of the situation.
Draw a House Card: This will pinpoint the area affected.
Draw two cards from a combined stack of Elemental, Emphasis, and Blank Cards.
>**Elemental Card:** This will show you the challenges you must overcome and the lessons you must learn.
>**Emphasis Card:** These cards pinpoint the area to focus on and show whether the reading is Physical, Emotional, or Spiritual. All three apply, but one area may be predominant for the reading.
>**The Blank Cards:** These cards can be assigned positive values. You may use them or not. Do what you are comfortable with and what works for you. Do not assign any negative value to your Blank Cards or you will negate the power of the deck by allowing negative influences to infiltrate it.

If a blank card is drawn for a Planetary, House, Elemental, or Divinity Card in a reading, the area from which it is drawn does not play strongly into the reading and the rest of the draws should be read. You can draw again, but a more true reading results from the initial drawing.

An upside down card does not have any significance in The New Spirit Astrology System. The impetus behind The New Spirit Astrology System is positive and life affirming. The Elements provide the challenges we need to face and master to achieve the highest transformational levels we can reach for ourselves.

Keep the "Alternative Two" grouping as you drew it, and read on to find the correct chart. Your Planetary and House Cards are only in one place. Then read on about "How to Do a Full or Comprehensive Chart."

Other Uses for the Planetary, House, and Elemental Cards: The Planetary, House, and Elemental Cards can also be used for any specific question that is not of a negative nature and that is not asked for another person without permission. Pose the question clearly in your mind and say it three times or repeat the *threefold request*: "I ask this is in the perfect way, the perfect number of times." Re-pose the question as you shuffle the cards, and turn up the cards that "feel" or look right.

If a reading feels off or is wrong:

First Check: Did you switch a Sun 1, Moon 1 or Earth/Venus 1 with a Sun 2, Moon 2 or Earth/Venus 2 in your reading?

Check with the Divinity Cards to see what is going on. The cards "tune in" to the energy of the person handling the cards. If multiple people handle the cards, cleanse the cards between handlers. You may need to cleanse the cards and your stones (if you work in a stone circle) with the four Elements or incense.

HOW TO DO A FULL OR COMPREHENSIVE CHART

To Answer the question "What Cards Have Meaning for Me Now?"

First, understand the difference between a **Full** and a **Comprehensive** Chart. Additional information regarding Full and Comprehensive Charts can be found in the articles, "Advanced Guide to the Maximum Potential of the New Spirit Astrology System," on the website.

From two cards, a Planetary Card and House Card, you have access to twelve combinations which will give you a Full Chart.

Look at the Planetary Card and the House Card you have chosen in combination.

Example: You have chosen a Sun 2 Planetary Card and a House 9 numeric card.

FROM JUST THESE TWO CARDS YOU CAN DETERMINE YOUR FULL CHART by finding the correct chart that includes the combination you drew. Scan the charts to find Sun 2, House 9. This combination is located in the first chart, "Basis Chart 1." All twelve of the Planet and House placements in the Basis Chart 1 grouping make up your Full Chart.

You can stop here, or go on to compile your Comprehensive Chart using the remaining cards.

To Complete a Comprehensive Chart, make a third stack of the Elements, Emphasis, and Blank Cards and **shuffle these cards.**

Turn up only two cards. You may get two blanks or some combination of Elements and Emphasis and Blanks. The first card is the Level 1, Earthly lesson, and the second card is the Level 2, spiritual lesson.

> Elemental Cards. These are the Elemental influences that are guiding you at this stage of your Lifescript, or Life Plan.
>
> **The Elemental Cards describe challenges we need to overcome and lessons we need to learn.**
>
> **Find the Element you drew in the Elements section of the book.** If you have turned up two Elemental Cards, remember, the first card will be the Earthly challenges, Level 1 Element. A second Elemental Card will be the transformational higher-self Level 2 Element.
>
> **Blank Cards.** **If you draw a blank first**, the reading is telling you that only the other card is significant and you are only working with the other card which is in a Level 2 placement.
>
> > **If you draw an Element or Emphasis card first**, it is in the Level 1 Earthly challenge placement and the Blank is the Level 2 placement.
> >
> > **If you drew two blanks**, the Elements or Emphasis Cards aren't significant in this particular reading.
>
> Emphasis Cards. You may pull one or two. Emphasis Cards fine-tune your reading and give you an indication as to whether the reading is primarily Physical, Emotional, or Spiritual. Note the placement to determine if it is a Level 1 (Earthly) or Level 2 (Higher-Self). Find the Emphasis section of the book and read the selection describing the card you pulled.

Divinity Cards. The Divinity Cards are six cards that can be used alone or as a check or reinforcement of the message you have received. Again, shuffle the Divinity Cards, use the *threefold request or state instead*: "I ask this question in the perfect way, the perfect number of times." Use these cards at any time.

Regarding the Divinity Cards, remember not to ask two questions in one. Use "computer logic." If you say, for example, "Can you tell me if I should go to Spain?" you have asked a confusing question. The answer might be "Yes," but "Yes" doesn't mean you should go to Spain. It means, "Yes, I can tell you."

If the response, "It is not to your highest good to answer at this time" is drawn, be assured that the answer was given and it will be revealed at the proper time to your spiritual development. The answer is there to be retrieved when you are ready to hear it or when you need it.

RESTING ORDER

This is very important!

When you are finished with your reading, regroup and store the cards in this resting order:

Blank Card

Planets 1-12

Blank Card

Houses 1-12

Blank Card

Elements 1-6

Blank Card

Emphasis Cards 1-3

Blank Card

Divinity 1-6

Remaining Blank Card

The cards are numbered; however, the six Blank Cards aren't numbered. Initially, the Blank Cards are used as front and back cover and separation cards between groups for the natural order of the deck. However, if there is a major Divinity aspect that you work with all the time and you wish to assign some positive and life affirming value to the cards, by all means do so, and then permanently mark that card and include that card or cards in with your Divinity section.

EASY GRAPH CHART

If you've drawn a Planetary Card, look for its name on the left (watch your ones and two's).

If you've drawn a House Card, read the numbers.

Whatever is at the top beside Sun 1 (bold larger numbers) in the crossed column is the full chart number.

Example:

You drew a **Sun 2 Planetary Card** and a **House of Karma, 12th House Card**.

Find Sun 2 on the left side of the chart and scan across that line looking for a 12 – that's House 12.

Follow that column to the top Sun 1.

Sun 1 is in the 4th House of the Subconscious.

Subconscious Chart 4 is the correct chart to go to to find your two-card draw and that chart is your Full Chart.

Sun 1	1		2		3		4	
Moon 1	2		3		4		5	
Earth/Venus 1	3		4		5		6	
Mars	4		5		6		7	
Neptune	5		6		7		8	
Saturn	6		7		8		9	
Uranus	7		8		9		10	
Minerva	8		9		10		11	
Sun 2	9		10		11		12	
Moon 2	10		11		12		1	
Earth/Venus 2	11		12		1		2	
Mercury	12		1		2		3	

Sun 1	5		6		7		8	
Moon 1	6		7		8		9	
Earth/Venus 1	7		8		9		10	
Mars	8		9		10		11	
Neptune	9		10		11		12	
Saturn	10		11		12		1	
Uranus	11		12		1		2	
Minerva	12		1		2		3	
Sun 2	1		2		3		4	
Moon 2	2		3		4		5	
Earth/Venus 2	3		4		5		6	
Mercury	4		5		6		7	

Sun 1	9		10		11		12	
Moon 1	10		11		12		1	
Earth/ Venus 1	11		12		1		2	
Mars	12		1		2		3	
Neptune	1		2		3		4	
Saturn	2		3		4		5	
Uranus	3		4		5		6	
Minerva	4		5		6		7	
Sun 2	5		6		7		8	
Moon 2	6		7		8		9	
Earth/ Venus 2	7		8		9		10	
Mercury	8		9		10		11	

FULL CHART READINGS

To find the correct starting point for Sun 1:

> Find your two-card draw in the previous charts (Planet on the left and the House numbers on the right).
>
> Move your eyes straight up to the Sun 1 top line on the previous charts.
>
> Or
>
> Find your two-card draw in the Table of Contents and look in the parentheses for the correct Chart number.

BASIS CHART 1

1. Sun 1
2. Moon 1
3. Earth/Venus 1
4. Mars
5. Neptune
6. Saturn
7. Uranus
8. Minerva
9. Sun 2
10. Moon 2
11. Earth/Venus 2
12. Mercury

This chart is the natural order chart, the chart of the Sun's birth.

Sun 1 in the 1st House of Basis: These people are beloved of Spirit and blessed throughout their lifetimes with direct communication with the Creator and all his creations. If they remain balanced, open, and receptive, they will hear direct guidance from above. They must work hard to fulfill Spirit's directives. The harder they try, successful or not, the greater the happiness afforded in this blessed existence.

Moon 1 in the 2nd House of Value: These people will have difficulty holding onto money because they love to buy things for their home, families, and friends. They buy for the pleasure of buying and giving. They want things around them that actually mean something. They will put up pictures and take them down when they are bored with them. The real secret is that they don't like things to stay the same. They love a look that can change on a whim, with colored pillows, bed covers, drapes, and rugs. If they could change the wall colors without the work involved, they would do that too.

They are inclined to gamble and take chances financially. In all probability, they will make and lose several fortunes in their lifetimes. The Spiritual Test for them, however, is to get their spiritual priorities in line and learn to value family and self first. They must, at this stage of the transformation, begin to practice a "give-away" mentality and stop spending money long enough to begin curbing their accumulation of material goods. The priority is to gather people together, not things.

Earth/Venus 1 in the 3rd House of Conscious Mind: Earth/Venus 1 Beings are grounded in the reality of loving, caring relationships, and it is unlikely that they will stay with anyone who doesn't reciprocate that love or that they will allow any kind of abuse. They will insist on being themselves and immediately try to improve everyone else around them. They can be exasperating in this regard, but they are deeply loved by their family. They will always champion the ones they love. The children of these people will know, beyond the shadow of a doubt, that they are loved. They are shown love in every way, and family life will be comfortable and generally happy.

Mars in the 4th House of Subconscious Mind: People with this placement will always be a champion for the underdog. They will be a champion even when that underdog won't fight for themselves, nor does that underdog necessarily want a champion. The underdogs just want to go along and get along without rocking the boat and won't appreciate the boat being rocked, even under the guise of help they desperately wish they had the nerve to ask for or gripe about not having. It will take many life experiences to understand that some people just like to be victims, and even if the fight is won for them, those people will sabotage things somehow so they can remain victims. Boring. Once the people with Mars in the Subconscious mind accept this, they can drop the superman cape and find people worthy of help. These Mars Beings have had many lifetimes of fighting battles for people who have appreciated a warriors' help. The true test for people with this placement is not to help unless asked.

Neptune in the 5th House of Love Aspect: These people, although basically lovable, will have a very hard time believing that someone can actually love them. It is always a little surprising that someone can see through all of the barriers the vulnerable Neptunians will put up to protect themselves. Even if they open themselves sufficiently to accept that another mate "might" really love them, they will push the partner's love as far as they can to see if it can be broken. There aren't a lot of people who can understand this treatment of their love. This isn't low self-esteem. It's a basic mistrust. If the love interest rises to the challenge, the Neptune Beings become increasingly secure in the knowledge that they are actually loved. The saving grace is that if the love interest stays long enough for the Neptune Beings to accept that they are loved, and loved completely and utterly, then they will relax and just enjoy being loved. The Spiritual Test for this aspect, however, is to deserve the love that they test so indiscriminately and learn to respect that playing games with basic trust and their loved ones' tender hearts may backfire, alienating those they do love.

Saturn in the 6th House of Physical Aspect: Peel an onion and you get layers and layers of onion. Peel the personal perception of people with Saturn in the 6th House of Physical Aspect and you get changeable layers of personality that barely resemble each other. These Saturnians are perfect chameleons and make excellent super spies. They love exposing different layers of the variety of personalities that make them so expertly adaptable and are likely to also change their hair color and clothing more often than a Broadway actor. As they get older, their self-perception may not match their outward appearance at all. They may have to give up stiletto heels or sandals for walking shoes, but they see themselves in stilettos and sandals. They will have certain outfits that evoke happy memories and may dress in an eccentric manner, insisting on wearing their "happy hats" or lucky shirt. They remain forever young and forever playful. When they change their make-up and hairstyle, they change their outlook, but not necessarily their viewpoint. Their new style will reflect in a brighter outlook, a fresh perspective, and a happier view. Halloween will be one of their favorite holidays. Maybe the only day they allow themselves to show this side of themselves. Watch out!

Uranus in the 7th House of Emotional Aspect: Emotions here can change from ecstatic to gloomy in the blink of an eye. These folks process everything, worry about everything, and face a hard life lesson if they can't learn to go with the flow more. When they do smile, their whole body smiles, and it is a beautiful thing. They **want** to be happy; they just rarely stay that way for very long. They can depress themselves quite easily or let their happy moments be ruined by somebody else's innocent remark or action. These beings can be gloomy and negative, and it will be a lifelong battle to find some peaceful middle ground. The Spiritual Test here is for them to take a deep breath, just stop processing, and practice counting their blessings. They just need to enjoy the moment and try to live more fully, letting the little things go. They need to learn the knack of picking their battles and practice not deliberately causing discord over everything, taking on only the very important issues, and learning to give the other guy his way sometimes. Uranus in this aspect basically wants to be happy and wants others to be happy too. Everyone can be!

Minerva in the 8th House of Generation: Minervan Beings are living in a state of transformation from the physical to the spiritual and this makes for a rough and confusing physical life. They are always operating with one step off the planet and moving toward their personal transformational path and toward oneness with Spirit. Because of direct spiritual contact with the Creator, Minervans are also receiving a constant stream of "data" that makes dream states and fantasy very real for them on many levels. They are often asked to help Spirit on the astral, dream, and physical planes, and unless these people can hold it together to live these secret lives in the midst of day to day reality, they may be seen as highly eccentric. They will probably doubt their own sanity. It should help to know why they feel as they do. If they will use the gifts given and own them, they will live a more normal life. The Spiritual Test for these beings is to understand that they are blessed of Spirit and as such are expected to help when they are asked; and they will be asked.

Sun 2 in the 9th House of Regeneration: The Sun 2 Beings with this placement are given spiritual protection and guidance throughout their lives and are already transformed. They have chosen to return from the Soulforce Pool to Earth to accomplish tasks set for them by Spirit. The trick in this lifetime is to accept that they are doing Spirit's work on Earth and may have to accept that others may not understand this. These people are Angels on Earth and maybe more, but unless that is accepted, then it is a wasted gift. They must act, in whatever fashion they can, upon the direction given. In return, they get the gift of having physicality again and can enjoy sensory touch and smells, a good meal, a happy healthy home, and loved ones. They may also be expected to heal the sick or work with the energy matrix of the Universe to heal the Universe too. They can do the work quietly and alone with the help of a few like minded friends, even if the friends are rocks, animals, or planets. The Sun is the revitalizing force for Sun 2 Beings, and they can channel the necessary energy and instruction from there to do what is asked. The Spiritual Test is to stay balanced and listen for instructions from a quiet voice surrounded by white light.

Moon 2 in the 10th House of Universal Lifeforce: First of all, congratulations, Moon People, for making it this far. This isn't an easy aspect for anyone. In this position, they are asked to switch major gears and go for Lifeforce training almost exclusively, facing the toughest test yet for their tender hearts. They have to learn that love does not come without sacrifice, and direct action is sometimes required to protect another. They have to grow up spiritually and make themselves get off the fence to act if an innocent is threatened with harm. This is tough love in more ways than one because while a Lifeforce aspect is a little harsher and colder than a Loveforce aspect, in truth it is necessary for survival.

The other spiritual task for the higher-self of these beings is to do some soul searching for their next incarnation. The Moon is the dominion of Diana and the Venuvians, and their task is to help souls transit after death to their next incarnation. Whatever challenges we set for ourselves in our Lifescripts (our next life's plan) we are solely the ones who decide the path. The Lifescript is complex. We agree to be father, mother, sister, brother, wife, husband, son, or daughter, and we coordinate with the souls who wish to work with us in this incarnation.

What this translates to in the Earthly incarnation is that people with this aspect may be powerfully confused. They will sometimes feel like an alien in a touchy feely world that they no longer can identify with, and consequently, they may have some personal issues in relationships. Take heart. This is a tough lifetime, but eventually things will start falling into place and some peace can be reached. How? It's a miracle!

Earth/Venus 2 in the 11th House of Universal Loveforce: The people who draw these two cards or have them in their full or comprehensive charts have big responsibilities. They are being tasked by Spirit to advocate not only for the health of Mother Earth, but also the health of all the planets in all solar systems. These Earth/Venus Beings will be working nightly with Spirit to affect universal Balance. The higher souls of these individuals are also tasked with helping other souls transition from their Earthly bodies to their spiritual bodies, helping them discern which Life Path lessons and challenges they must face if they must reincarnate. This requires Archangel status on Earth. These Earth/Venus 2 Beings have earned their souls, and have chosen to return to Earth to help others earn theirs. They work with the Fleur d'leis,* those entities chosen by Spirit to assist them in healing and teaching on Earth. The Spiritual Tests have been passed, and this soul may move on to the Soulforce pool at any point in their reincarnations. They have what Spirit calls, "earned increment," which is spiritual blessing, protection, and guidance directly from the Creator.

Mercury in the 12th House of Karma: Mercury people have experienced many charmed existences in their incarnations. When they incarnate enough times to reach this point, they are preparing to join the Soulforce Pool and stop the incarnations. They will have the ultimate journey home. All the traveling and the restless absorption with keeping moving will finally make sense as worldly endeavors come to a halt and spiritual endeavors ensue. Mercury has been a messenger, and if he has learned anything, it's that people often want to kill the messenger. This, unfortunately, stops many Mercurial people in their spiritual paths. They get discouraged when the messages they are trying to deliver just aren't being received, but if Mercury people have been listening closely, Spirit has been telling them to "endeavor to persevere" because the Earth is dependent upon its messengers for continued survival. Friends and family of Mercury people at this juncture seem to be secondary to the driving need to fulfill a messenger's higher duty and loved ones will either understand, or Mercury people will do what they need to do without the support of friends and family. The charming Mercurial children have grown up and they have important work to do.

*Fleur d'leis explanation: People think this is a misspelling, when really it is an older spelling of the term, which means, "Flower of Lifeforce" in the stone or Pen'l Leina-Language. What this involves is a deep look at and cleansing of any residual hatreds or a sense of things left undone, in order to forgive, forget, or let go and move on. These beings will have Physical, Emotional, and Spiritual Tests to pass. The book, *Spirit Speaks-the Transformation Connection,* channeled in part to Johan Adkins, gives very specific instructions on how to find out where you are on this journey. The Fleur d'leis teaching is also available there. When people achieve this status, a lot changes. They feel an increased awareness; they can move energy in any direction; they have the ability to hear and see Spirit; and they have increased ability to work with the Elements, Vortex, and the creatures of Earth, sea, and sky and deal with negative energy and transmute or destroy it if necessary. Their skill at creative visualization is extremely powerful, and their higher selves can literally create what they imagine for the Universe. This requires mature and forward-thinking analysis of the situation. Their abilities to heal all things will increase, and they will have an innate understanding of what to do. They will really earn their spiritual symbol of the fleur de lys. This traditional French symbol represents many things, but historically it is a symbol of protection and honor.

VALUES CHART 2

- 2   Sun 1
- 3   Moon 1
- 4   Earth/Venus 1
- 5   Mars
- 6   Neptune
- 7   Saturn
- 8   Uranus
- 9   Minerva
- 10   Sun 2
- 11   Moon 2
- 12   Earth/Venus 2
- 1   Mercury

Sun 1 in the 2nd House of Value: To keep peace, this is the key to understanding life with Sun Beings in the House of Values. In a relationship, or in the workplace, if someone who is supposed to be an equal power and partner attempts to make unilateral decisions, ANY unilateral decisions, there will be discord. Period. An important life lesson for the Sun in the House of Values people is to pick their battles and prioritize what is truly important to them, learning to let others have their way sometimes. A Spiritual Lesson here is to learn to listen and work on grace and control issues.

Take heart. All is not lost as long as the partner or workmates of these Sun Beings remain strong. If there is love and/or respect, all parties can agree to disagree and work to find a happy medium on just about everything. Sun Beings crave harmony and balance; however, they instigate matters constantly that cause disharmony. Their Spiritual Test is to learn to value the opinions and feelings of others by practicing complete silence and learning to listen without feeling the need to fix everything and everybody.

Moon 1 in the 3rd House of Conscious Mind: Female energies are behind everything here. A male with this placement will have an innate understanding of women and his fashion sense should be relied upon. He is one male, who when his female friend asks, "Does this dress make my butt look big?" will respond, "Yes! Take it off!" The really great thing about his honesty is that he will have something in hand to give her that will make her look absolutely fabulous; and guaranteed: her butt won't look big. This fashion sense extends for both male and female into a great sense of décor and design in their homes, including a loving, warm environment there too.

Both sexes will make their families and workmates confront whatever issues need resolving right away. These people will have to guard against molding themselves to their partners' personalities to the point that they lose their own. It is a Spiritual Transformational Test in this placement: Moon Beings must learn not to change who they are for anybody. If someone loves them, they need to love them for who they really are and any attempt to "fix" or change them has to be dealt with. If evolved, Moon Beings will deal with this as they deal with everything else: bring it out into the light and address the issue right there.

Earth/Venus 1 in the 4th House of Subconscious Mind: Earth and Venus Beings aren't very comfortable with hiding stuff. Love is kind; but to not keeping some things hidden would be unkind. Brutal honesty is just that…brutal, and it is unnecessary. If there is any lesson Loveforce needs, it is how to hold that tripping tongue and not "tell all," especially when telling may hurt the ones we love. The answer to "Have you ever loved anyone more than you love me?" is always "No, I love you with all of my heart and want to spend the rest of my life with you, Darling." It is never, "Oh hell yeah! I would have married Brad Pitt in a minute if he had asked me first."

The Spiritual Test for these Beings is to think of the consequences of truth for others before indulging in the basic selfish need to have everything on the table, regardless of whom it hurts. These beings need to care so much about others that the pain of holding that tripping tongue is their pain, to be carried within, and not borne by others because of a need to speak. One can be truthful without causing pain. Diplomacy is the lesson here.

Mars in the 5th House of the Love Aspect: Warriors can love. They can love their country and their fellow military brothers or sisters and possibly a mate, but the hardest test is to believe that they themselves are worthy of love. They must learn to love themselves first and then that love can extend to others. Because of a fierce individualistic lifestyle and mentality, Mars lovers may be very difficult to love. They may place barriers in the way of finding love and once it is found, they will feel a need to see if it can be destroyed by tests at ridiculous levels. Loving Mars Beings is never easy, but it is worth the effort if you can resist killing them.

Neptune in the 6th House of the Physical Aspect: Because Saturn is the planet whose underlying power affects this placement, these Neptunians are more outgoing and confident than other people. They are just "more." There are energies at play that give them the confidence necessary to get exactly what they want and need. If you find yourself in this placement, you will be that person with just a little more chutzpah: the one people notice and listen to. They will want to help you because you're going to make it seem like the great idea you're talking about was theirs all along! So put on that cape of invincibility and go for it!

Saturn in the 7th House of the Emotional Aspect: Generally, Saturns have a lot of self-confidence. They can speak in public and get on the stage and shine, but these Saturn Beings face the possibility of obstacles placed in the way by Uranus' heavy energies. The Uranus energy underlying this aspect will make things just a little bit harder and more confusing for the Saturnians in this aspect. They should expect to experience not only a heightened level of perception here but also some elevation of fears and trepidations. Dreams may be more intense than usual. This represents a possible run of bad luck that may have to be addressed if this placement appears for you. Things that are usually easy will come hard because the Uranus' challenge is to learn from mistakes and become self-aware, understanding that they alone are ultimately responsible for themselves and their own perceptions. So here psychic abilities will be tested. A cleansing and balancing visualization to help keep clarity and light in your world can remove this negativity, but don't be afraid of it. You control what happens here and nobody else. Keep in mind that you have Spirit's direction in this challenge and there are lessons to be learned. This can be a blessing if you are cleansed and balanced because you will be given a door to experience what psychics and holy people who commune with Spirit experience. Faery sight is at the edge of your awareness and all you have to do is balance, cleanse, and open the third eye to see. Watch, study, listen, and be amazed.

Uranus in the 8th House of Generation: The House of Generation tells Uranians where they are on their transformational path; it also tells them the way things are, not the way they would like them to be. Minerva, the underlying energy behind this sign, puts a pretty heavy load on the night life of Uranus Beings: dream teaching, dreamweaving, and teaching the astral traveler how to walk outside of their bodies and in the bodies of their fellows. Uranus is expected to listen at this point and stay balanced and rested in order concentrate in night school.

If you've drawn this card to try to understand what is going on, then something or someone is seeming mysterious or out of place in your normal realm of understanding. Maybe you thought you understood the situation thoroughly and all of a sudden people are talking *Alienese* and somehow you missed the language lesson. What is probably happening is that you're not getting enough rest and/or the night school demands that Spirit is placing on your energies are wearing you down. A few naps and early bed nights should set you right and people will be talking your language very soon If Spirit or your family is making too many demands on your time or attention, talk (meditate, pray) to their higher selves and ask them to tell the physical bodies that you need them to back off to let you rest and regroup. You may think that this won't work for infants and children, but try it and you will be surprised. Talk to their little sleepy heads. They will get the message.

Minerva in the 9th House of Regeneration: What a neat place for Minervans to be! This is the House of potential to reach the highest level of transcendence, the level that allows us to be everything we can be. Minervans in this House have learned their dream work lessons and now can move on to help others. The people with this aspect will be dream masters. They will be able to direct their dreams and work inter-dimensionally and extra-dimensionally to help other Beings choose the right path in their spiritual journeys. When these people go to sleep, they go to work. If Minervan Beings are very well balanced, they will be gifted with remembering the work they have done. It can be very satisfying to live multi-dimensional lives.

If you've drawn this card in response to a question about people or situation, this may be what is happening: you are having dreams that seem so real that the people in them feel real too, as if they are precious long-time friends or family. You've stumbled onto one of your multi-dimensional lives. Having this experience will allow you to explore this further if you stay balanced. Don't be surprised if you revisit this dream and these people in the future. Ask for direction from your Divinity Cards and before sleeping, ask Spirit (three times) to help you understand what you need to do to help.

Sun 2 in the 10th House of Universal Lifeforce: Trust your instincts. This is the perfect balance of Lifeforce and Loveforce and as such, the understanding you will be given is nothing short of the voice of Spirit whispering in your ear and guiding your life. You are given spiritual guidance not only in your personal lives, but to help the Earth and your fellow beings. Notice, I said *beings*, not just humans. You are in a singular position to offer healing to the Earth, the creatures of the Earth, the rocks and water systems of the Earth, and the energy of everything. You are blessed with the gift of healing, and moving energy on a cellular or a universal level will be easy for you. The trick is to keep clear, keep good things in your body, and don't pollute the vessel of Spirit's work...you. What is offered is earned increment for the cause of love and healing. What you visualize you can create. Instruction and guidance and messages will come in dreams or waking visions. Trust your gifts.

Moon 2 in the 11th House of Universal Loveforce: People who have reached this point have buried their personal demons. They are influenced only by the need to help people understand that love must be the answer to the chaos of the world. Humankind will not survive unless we help one another, and this commitment goes deeper than Earthly love. It extends to a universal power of love and feminine energy with the power to right all wrongs. Men in this placement will be doing the same work as the women: they will be dynamic leaders for peace. They have fought the chaos within and have gained inner peace and wisdom; now they wish to extend that love by actively practicing what they preach. And preach they may. They will all be spiritual leaders in one form or another, even if that means they will live their lives quietly and silently. They will be working with the Universe to spread the energy and concept of love and fighting darkness where they find it. They are powerful spiritual warriors. They are all, in one sense or another, universal prophets for love.

Earth/Venus 2 in the 12th House of Karma: Everything in this chart indicated that people with this placement have been given a larger task in this incarnation than that of personal transformation. They have to fight the fight for Earth, for the survival of the human race, and for the survival of the creatures of inner Earth as well as for those upon her surface and in her skies. They must also shoulder the task of protecting Mother Earth in her transformation as well. For this work they are given healing aspects and direct contact with the energy of Earth and the voice of Spirit.

What is dreamed can become reality, so dreams in this aspect will eventually take on visionary qualities, as these beings are also tasked with possibly traveling the Earth (physically and astrally) to spread the message to love. Their message is simple: stop hurting the Mother. The pollution needs to stop. The over-mining of her resources needs to stop. Crops must be diversified so that the world doesn't go hungry. These beings will know what is right in certain areas as they travel or visualize, and they will instinctively know what needs healing. They will experience a feeling of distress or wrongness when they come upon it. Their spiritual task is to tune in to the needs of Earth and actively address those needs. It is incumbent upon these people to heal these areas with light work or creative visualization of wellness. What can be imagined can be made manifest.

Mercury in the 1st House of Basis: People with Mercury in the House of Basis will be fun loving, adventurous, and great friends. They love life, and their families will include friends who are practically family. They also love freedom, and they don't like to be tied down to a schedule, to a commitment, or to a loved one. The person who is the mate to one of these individuals must be very social, somewhat mercurial, and up for anything at anytime, or at least willing and able to give their mates the freedom to be this way.

There's more going on than just fun and games with Mercury Beings. They have a very rich and comprehensive dream life. If they can manage to be balanced, they will be receiving instruction directly from their dreams. Mercury Beings have affiliations to Metal and like their namesake Mercury, they are fluid, flowing, and changeable. Their personalities, although gregarious and outgoing in all probability, do not reflect the true faces of these individuals. These people have big responsibilities to Spirit to be messengers, and because they don't really like having to be responsible to anyone, not even to Spirit, they must perhaps spend some time on a spiritual journey or quest to help themselves come to terms with what they must be willing to do.

CONSCIOUS MIND CHART 3

3	Sun 1
4	Moon 1
5	Earth/Venus 1
6	Mars
7	Neptune
8	Saturn
9	Uranus
10	Minerva
11	Sun 2
12	Moon 2
1	Earth/Venus 2
2	Mercury

Sun 1 in the 3rd House of Conscious Mind: We are not individual beings. We are energy beings given a body in order to enjoy the physicality of Earthly life. Nothing is as it seems on the one hand but on the other hand, Sun Beings in the House of Conscious Mind have a unique perspective on loneliness and they understand both male and female energies within themselves and in their partners. Happily, this understanding extends universally to everything and everybody. As a result of a very balanced id, they will be able to confidently shop with the girls or play softball with the boys, whether they are male or female. They will advocate for equality on every front and will be the most understanding parents in the world. Their capacity for love and caring and nurturing knows no boundaries.

Moon 1 in the 4th House of Subconscious Mind: Even really great mothers, fathers, daughters, sons, and mates get frustrated sometimes, and the hidden part of us has very few acceptable outlets to release the pent up anger and frustration we feel. So what do we do with these feelings if we can't express them? We handle the little things as they come up to try to keep them from escalating into big things. We're honest with our responses within the parameter of doing no harm, but we have to learn to stop saying, "I'm okay, I'm okay, I'm okay" when we really are not. Spirit tries to help us with this in dreamstate lessons that show us the need to respect ourselves, ask for what we need and want when we need it, and if necessary, be willing to fight for whatever is required. That's a big deal with some of us. We give, but we don't take back. The deeper lesson here is to learn reciprocity.

Earth/Venus 1 in the 5th House of Love Aspect: Love is the driving force behind all three energies at work here. Earth/Venus Beings are traditionally motherly, natural, and comfortable in their skin. Earthly love, and the Earth part of these Beings, love the closeness of sexual encounters. Venus contributes mature love and a willingness to fight and sacrifice for innocents. The underlying influence of Neptune adds the illusive and mysterious love that puts the self first. All of the influences of these powerhouse feminine planets would seem to make this a hard aspect for a man to handle, but a man in this placement will have an innate understanding of women and the feminine, and a gift for sexual pleasure. Both males and females with this aspect will be totally at ease with their with bodies and sex will be like food: necessary and satisfying. This is a happy, loving mix of energies, and the Sun-Creator energy can always step in with Lifeforce energy if the shopping gets out of hand. The true test of this placement is to extend the overabundance of love to the Universe. Teach love, live love, and show others, by example, just how powerful Loveforce can be.

Mars in the 6th House of Physical Aspect: Combine the physical aspects of two dynamic energies of Mars with Saturn as the background energy influence here, and you get beautiful and dynamic. Men with this placement will be brooding, complicated, fascinating, sexy, charming, and illusive; women will be knock-out gorgeous and also brooding, complicated, fascinating, sexy, charming, and illusive. It won't matter how old these people get, how many pounds they put on, or how thin or gray their hair becomes, their inner hunks or bombshells will forever shine through. If there is any doubt, just wait until they smile at you!

The challenges these beings face involve keeping their tempers and their mood swings under control, and ultimately, over the years, they will learn to do so. However, raising children who have this aspect can be interesting. Moms and dads of these tikes must be able to give them a lot of love and understanding. The Spiritual Tests for these Mars Beings are to learn to stay grounded, listen, and try to learn to empathize with others. Their psychic gifts may give them a complete preview of another person's opinion or message, but it's important to allow others to talk anyway, even though they might already know everything that person wants to say.

Neptune in the 7th House of Emotional Aspect: Merfolk have always been depicted as beautiful men and women whose siren song seduced sailors to the sea only to drown them. There is a reason behind that myth. Neptune aspects represent sexuality, promiscuity, and destructive behavior in whatever House they show up in. Here it is in the House of Emotion. Even more potentially problematic is the fact that Neptune is weighed too heavily with Loveforce energy and is inherently imbalanced to Lifeforce energy. This adds a tendency for narcissism into the mix. Uranus' powerhouse energy in combination with Neptune in this aspect can also amplify that narcissism significantly. What we see here are people who could very easily love only themselves, play the field indefinitely, flit from relationship to relationship, and possibly spread destruction and unhappiness in a wide swath via their sexual endeavors.

Take heart. There is a way out of the trap of alienated friends and family, loves lost, and one night stands. The Transformational Test of this aspect is to give of yourself in service to another. Make someone else happy.

Saturn in the 8th House of Generation: Saturn Beings have a different and multi-dimensional skew on everything. They think quickly and so far outside the box that it is scary. In the House of Generation, Minerva sits as the mutable power behind this aspect, shifting the energy wherever it needs to go for the good of the Saturn Beings and the work they are trying to do for Spirit. Minerva's purview is dreamstate teaching and astral travel. Saturn Beings will be going to night school and using their additional gifts of psychic perception and dimensional thinking to deal with universal problems. This is a think-tank aspect and in it, Saturn Beings will be bringing a great deal to the spiritual table. If they stay balanced and focused, they may be more tired during periods of normal rest, work, and play on Earth but it will be a satisfying kind of tired after accomplishing a job well done on the universal level. Saturn Beings have the maturity at this point of their spiritual evolution to be able to control the psychic babble and fine-tune their gifts and skills. This is an exciting and dynamic opportunity to create a fine balance in life and for Saturn Beings to gain the confidence that they can do anything!

Uranus in the 9th House of Regeneration: Spirit has a lot of hope for Uranus Beings. They have really been "through it." For them to get to this point, they have been through hard Spiritual Tests through eight previous aspects and have met the challenges. Now, the big gun, Sun 2, the Creator energy, is backing them up to assure their best possible chance of moving farther down the transformational path successfully. They have two more aspects to go, even if it has taken hundreds of lives to get here! Uranus has twenty times the

Lifeforce/Loveforce energy, and these beings traditionally set very hard tasks for themselves in their Life Path plans. The Planet Uranus has taken on the reputation of being the Planet that provides obstacles. Uranus Beings, like determined and faithful drill sergeants, choose to put themselves and others through the paces. The reward for success, however, is great.

There is a hierarchy in Spirit, and one of the most sought after placements in the Soulforce Pool is that of the Creator's trusted inner guard: the Walkers. Uranus Beings aspire to earn status here because it means that they will literally be powerful enough to shift energy from planet to planet or mend the matrix of the Universe with a thought. They seek to do something else as well: help other war weary and tortured souls find peace. The way they do this is by understanding, more than any other being, what it means to fight alone against incredible odds. These are the Spirit Guides of soldiers and protectors. Once Uranus Beings transcend from this point, Spirit has special tasks for them as they finally earn their place in the Soulforce Pool: either returning as Angels on Earth to help others in their transformational paths or joining the Soulforce Pool to actively work to balance the Universes. Uranus will be Metal affiliated, and that's a big deal. They will be able to join the Creator in journeys to repair the matrix that holds the Universe together. The Spiritual Test for the 9th House is for Uranus Beings to stay balanced male to female and start working in their higher selves in dreamstate in night school with the Metal Elementals and Vortex.

Minerva in the 10th House: Spirit requires that the people in this aspect be balanced male to female. Minerva, being mutable, is almost always balanced male to female, so that's one test completed. Minervans also have the guidance of the trinity to help them accomplish Lifeforce training. This must be done in dreamtime or in literally walking a mile in another's shoes. It requires that the individuals be adept at "walking" in another; experiencing and perceiving how others feel; looking beyond appearances to what something or somebody else is actually experiencing at some given moment. It requires that Minervans be hyper aware of everything around them and active in helping any other entities (animals, Spirit, plant people, Elementals) who need help regardless of whether they have been asked to do so. It requires that help be offered so that those needing guidance, advice, or help can learn to accept it gracefully. At this point in the growth of the soul, these people are literally acting as Angels on Earth to assist Spirit to help others accomplish the goals they have set for themselves in their Lifescripts. The Spiritual Test is to become selfless in this regard to help other entities attain their goals. Spirit's message is this: trust the instinct to lend a hand and don't be embarrassed if the offer of help is rejected. Spirit is also testing the entity that refuses your help. You provided the lesson, but they failed to accept direct spiritual intervention.

Sun 2 in the 11th House of Universal Loveforce: This is a big picture aspect, and it is also a big blessing. It is very possible that the people with this placement will be called to spread the message of love and Spirit's teachings to great groups of people. Alternately, they may choose to live their lives in quiet anonymity, simply enjoying the blessing of direct spiritual contact and universal teaching. No matter which road they choose, in this aspect these Sun 2 Beings are blessed with direct contact from a higher form, or lots of higher forms, depending on their belief systems. They are given an understanding of the lessons of universal love, joy, and peace. All they have to do to enjoy this blessing is to fully stay balanced in every way, listen, and live their lives in such a way that makes them able to hear.

Moon 2 in the 12th House of Karma: Mercury is an underlying energy in the House of Karma. On the positive side, Mercury is travel and adventure; on the negative side, escapism. With Moon's water influence here and the fact that Mercury is liquid metal, this escape from reality might easily become a flow into problems with drugs, alcohol, or negative adventures into the Earthier side of sexuality or life.

If people with this placement will seek spiritual guidance from the feminine side of themselves or their friends or family, they can stay on track in their transformational journey. The upside is that Moon's influence of Loveforce/Lifeforce energies is strong enough to overcome Mercury's negative possibilities. However, there will be immediate karma for any action that works against the higher good of these individuals or their friends and family members. The upside is that Moon's influence of Loveforce/Lifeforce energies can overcome Mercury's allure and karma works both ways. It can also bring about great blessings for great good. Love conquers all; it can conquer this too.

Earth/Venus 2 in the 1st House of Basis: Loveforce is the basis for Venus energy and the personality in this placement, but the key to these people's own well-balanced spirituality is to temper love with Lifeforce, the basis of the natural planet of this placement, the Sun. They will be tested regarding how deeply they can love unconditionally. The critical lesson for them is to learn that Loveforce alone is not enough because it is ultimately self-serving. There must always be Lifeforce involved as well to teach those whose basis for life is primarily Loveforce. While they may choose to turn their own cheek out of a sense of non-violence and peace, when the intent of others becomes abusive, they need to either flee or fight back. They especially need to protect those who cannot or will not protect themselves. Spirit's message is very clear. Care enough about yourselves and others not to accept harm or abuse. Run if you can, but be ready to fight back if you have to.

On a more positive note, these people will be the family glue. They will hold their families together with love, and are best suited to teaching a loving aspect to their spouses and children. They will be the ones who can always be relied upon in a crisis to be the loving hands and the caring individuals. Their love is deep and abiding.

Mercury in the 2nd House of Values: This is interesting. Here we have the positive side of the fluidity of Mercury Beings; the travelers and the dreamers in the House of Values, which represents money, family commitment, home values, marital relationships and children This combination won't be what you might expect. Mercury people can attract money like a magnet, or they can use a magnet to find money. They will be the people who look down and find $10.00 on the sidewalk. Who knew that they would be so talented in finance? They will probably make more money taking the kind of chances that no sane person would ever attempt, and when they try to give money away, they'll make even more. As to families, they may have one, but not have a clue what to do with it except play with it and have adventures. They won't be the typical parents. They will encourage their children to walk the rooftops and swim in deep water; they are prepared to rescue them, of course, but maybe not until they've broken an arm or almost drowned learning how to sink or swim. They will either have mates who are as understanding as only soul mates can be, as necessary as food to these mercurial individuals, or they will not be married at all. They will, in all likelihood have lots of flings and affairs before marriage. Mercury Beings, once committed, are faithful.

They don't like responsibilities of any kind, and the "honey do list" will get cobwebs on it from where it was chucked in the corner. They will provide amply for their families but will rarely stick around home with them. But when they *are* home, they are there 100%. The time they do give to their family has real substance to it. The time they give to *anything* has to have substance or they won't give it all. Most of the time though, they will be out biking or socializing or walking alone on mountain-trails, picking up the spare $10.00 that they will find there.

SUBCONSCIOUS MIND CHART 4

4	Sun 1
5	Moon 1
6	Earth/Venus 1
7	Mars
8	Neptune
9	Saturn
10	Uranus
11	Minerva
12	Sun 2
1	Moon 2
2	Earth/Venus 2
3	Mercury

Sun 1 in the 4th House of Subconscious Mind: Behind these great men and women is a secret life that occasionally oozes out around the edges of happiness, in this case appearing as anger and alienation. The Sun 1 Beings in the fourth house have the warrior Planet Mars behind the scenes breeding the possibility of discontent. They are generally centered around the need to have personal freedom and bristle at having that freedom curtailed in any way. The Sun Beings here have an inexplicable need to run the other way once they have earned the love of another, even if the Sun Beings were the ones who pursued that love to begin with. But don't misunderstand. Their hearts beat steady and true, and they are fiercely loyal to those few when they actually love. Herein lies the problem. These Sun people go through a lot of partners and the motions of love without feeling what they think they should feel for a lifelong mate. They may resist being tied down by marriage with a vengeance and that is probably a good thing because it is possible they may stray. They are often alienated from those they love by being "high maintenance," flighty, and inconsistent, and they tend to sabotage relationships on purpose. Although they love people in general and sometimes indiscriminately, they are experimenting with tender hearts and will almost always put their own need for freedom above another's need for reciprocal love. The Spiritual Test for this aspect is for Sun Beings to take time to be alone and celibate for a good long time until they understand why they never seem to get what they need. Then ask themselves this question, "Do I give my partner what they need?"

Moon 1 in the 5th House of Love Aspect: You would think that Moon 1, Beings essentially "love" in the House of Love, would be the very epitome of loving human beings. They are and they aren't. The problem is that Neptune energy sits behind this aspect and tilts the love aspect to that of self-love. It will be a constant battle for Moon 1 Beings to evolve beyond that basic nature. Moon 1 people are really pretty hard to love. While they expect others to meet their needs, they rarely even consider meeting anyone else's. Don't get me wrong. Moon Beings feel a great deal of love for everything and everybody, but they are easily pleased with those who will feed their ego. Mates of Moon 1 Beings really need to understand that they need to give and pay attention to the Moon person.

If Moon Beings marry, they will, in all probability stay faithful; however, the need for admiration and sexual identity will result in a teasing and flirtatious demeanor. Lots of partners don't like or understand this, and Moon individuals play with fire by acting this way. In all honesty, they probably can't help it.

There is another aspect to the Loveforce here: Moon Beings do not outgrow the need to feel acceptance from their parental units. If they do not get unequivocal love and support from parents early on, they will always be searching for parental figures to provide these things. They will likely pursue older mates or hang on to older mentors, teachers, or professors long after it is reasonable to let them go.

The Spiritual Test is for Moon Beings to take a step back and rethink this whole need for constant reaffirmation of love. If you are a Moon person, try to see the loving things people do and learn to recognize the unspoken support and daily care that that express love too. It is extremely hard to step out of the self and "let go and trust Spirit," but that is exactly what must happen to transcend beyond this aspect.

Earth/Venus 1 in the 6th House of Physical Aspect: Earth and Venus know that what you see in the mirror looks good to you and when the underlying charisma of Saturn comes into the picture then what you see looks good to others too. Saturn energy adds a bit of naughty and nice to an otherwise serious demeanor. Earth and Venus have always enjoyed attention, but in this aspect they have the added confidence from Saturn to act on some of their dreams, like being able to get in front of a crowd to advocate for the health of the Planet, or in a lighter vein, to finally join that local theatrical group and ham it up in front of a crowd. One thing is true almost without exception: these beings can sing like heavenly Angels, and whether they do it in the bathroom or in a concert hall, music will be very important to them. Their children will complain that mom and dad sing about everything! I know now that my Aunt Lillian had this aspect. She used to sing her children awake every morning with a musical blessing for the day. The Transformational Test for this aspect is to extend a helping hand to those who may not have the confidence in their abilities or dreams. Help someone else shine.

Mars in the 7th House of Emotional Aspect: When people are angry, they can't think straight. Sometimes situations that could be handled reasonably escalate into an argument or fight that blows the initial problem way out of proportion, with disastrous results. The real dilemma lies in whatever is behind the anger. Often it isn't anger over any particular incident, but anger over something unspoken or misunderstood. The male aspects of Mars and Uranus both sit behind this aspect, and neither is particularly warm and fuzzy when it comes to emotions.

The key is to do the opposite of what you would normally do. Breathe, and then breathe again. Don't react. If you would normally scream and shout, leave the room, and don't return until your emotions are under control. One tool you can use is "the talking stick." Whoever holds it gets to talk without interruption until he or she finishes saying what they need and want to say, then the stick is passed on to the next person. Everyone else must sit quietly and listen respectfully until it is his or her turn to talk. We used the talking stick at my house when my kids were little and my son's anger surfaced inappropriately. I remember my son telling us once that his sister was a weed in his garden. Since she was bigger and taller than he was, she was taking all of his sunlight. The problem was obviously that he didn't feel like he was getting enough individual attention. The Mars Being, having anger issues, may just need the weeds in the garden to be quiet and listen to him too.

Neptune in the 8th House of Generation: Neptune has always had a hard time figuring out what the situation is, so this placement presents a challenge. Neptune's water affiliation causes people with this aspect to ebb and flow in their decision-making and the heavy Loveforce power structure confuses the issue further. They quite literally and figuratively can love everybody, male or female; it may not matter. They are constantly searching for an avenue to give the overwhelming love they feel to one person but they consistently fail to find the one true love to give it to. Their lives will not be structured and they will, in all probability, attempt to raise children in the same vein. This will cause problems in a marriage or relationship in which a child is being raised.

Whether encumbered by marriage or not, the Neptune Being may have no sexual discernment and feels no barriers to spreading love around. The difficulty is that Neptunians are perfectly happy getting the attention they crave and being free in their own minds. They see no advantage to molding themselves to fit anybody else's picture of an ideal mate, and they stubbornly refuse to be dammed up. They flow out and around and over and under, slipping and sliding until they are back into their own flow. The Spiritual Test for this being is a tough one. They will have to start off being alone and then learn to give some of their unbounded love to themselves before extending it to anybody else. Only an eventual period of celibacy can break the pattern of self-defeating love affairs and broken marriages and prevent the possible pain felt by the other tender souls who may love them but can't fully have them. If Neptune finds their true love, they may be faithful. Ass long as the mates recognize the Neptune Beings basic need for independence, everyone can be relatively happy. Neptune Beings will still be a challenge to understand and live with.

Saturn in the 9th House of Regeneration: Saturnians in this aspect can go either way in their transformational paths. More than any of the other planetary signs, Saturn people can hear Spirit all the time and that gets a bit overwhelming. They get so inured to the constant psychic chatter that they can't or won't pick out the important from the unimportant chatter which clearly becomes a problem for them. The disturbing thing that Saturn Beings don't like to own up to is that not only can they hear everything all at once from everything and everybody, but they can also see whom they are hearing. They most certainly can train themselves to see auras, or they have always seen them if they were balanced enough. Many of them don't transcend beyond this stage. They become a little afraid for their sanity, so they shut down completely in an attempt to salvage some shred of normalcy.

What has to happen in order for Saturnians to proceed down the transformational path is for them to ask for a quiet mind and "one voice," one guide that they can depend upon for trustworthy guidance. They need to be able to designate a direction to face to see one guide and that guide needs to be available in that specific direction at all times so that any spiritual transmissions can be verified with what is seen and heard. Ask for a threefold blessing of a quiet mind with a designated guide and it will be a godsend for this aspect. "There can be only one."

Uranus in the 10th House of Universal Lifeforce: These people have been through the worst already, and it must seem to them that no matter what they do, things usually run southward; but they should take heart. Spirit is watching the struggle and standing right at their shoulders with the big guns to help guide them. In this aspect, both the traditional male Sun 2 and feminine Moon 2 energies help pave the way by helping them break many lifetimes of negative patterns that result in the Life Lessons being repeated and getting harder each time because these lessons went unlearned. These people are finally learning so life will get easier. They are searching for the higher road and spiritual path. Spirit is whispering in their ears and for the first time, they can hear. Working for Uranus beings is their inherent balance of male to female. Relationships will be working better in this lifetime than ever before and difficulties can be handled. The spiritual search is ongoing, but now there is light at the end of the dark tunnel and these people are finally able to walk into the light.

Minerva in the 11th House of Universal Loveforce: Minerva is mutable energy, which molds itself to the individual needs of the astral traveler. Yes, it is dream teaching, but in this house, it is more dream molding: creating a reality for someone or something for the good of the Universe as a whole. Minerva is tasked to work with the Vortex who create our perception of physical life. Minerva in this aspect has earned the great gifts of shaping reality to meet the needs of the individual and of the Universal Loveforce.

If you've drawn this card, life just got a little more complicated. Loving one person or one family isn't enough anymore. Your love has exponentially blossomed into understanding universal love: love for everybody and everything. Loving things means protecting things, and the warrior Minerva is well suited to teach you this. Much of the work will be done in your sleep, so be sure to stay balanced in order to remember what you learn in night school. You aren't just visualizing. You are, on a multi-dimensional level, *creating* reality, so be careful what you wish.

Sun 2 the 12th House of Karma: Sun 2 people always exist with one foot on the planet and one foot off. In the pursuit of inner peace and spiritual growth, they may take that foot and leave everything and everybody behind. If their family is lucky, they will come back, but they won't be the same. Traveling and having time to reflect will answer some questions, but more questions will likely come up that require more time for answers. Those who love these individuals will have to understand their needs for the Spirit Quest even though the loved ones may be left behind, perhaps permanently. If it's any consolation, the Sun Beings' quest has nothing to do with their jobs, friends, or family. The quest is not pursued because of them or in spite of them, nor does it mean love is lost and that the Sun 2 Beings are looking for something or someone else. They are, in fact, looking for themselves.

Moon 2 in the 1st House of Basis: This placement is blessed with the power of perfect balance, but this can cause problems. Negative energy is drawn to positive energy. Moon energy is Loveforce and Sun energy is Lifeforce, and the balance of power between these two energies is constantly in flux in all combinations of Planets and Houses in relation to each other. In this instance, these Moon individuals have done a great deal of Universal Loveforce work and there is the potential for perfect balance of power IF these people remain balanced (male to female and Elementally). If these tireless workers in Loveforce energy are imbalanced, they will not only hear negative direction, but they may be attacked. In this placement, these Moon 2 people must learn metaphysical defense methods. The book, *Spirit Speaks-The Transformation Connection* by the author of The New Spirit Astrology System, Johan Adkins, goes into protection and negative elimination methods, and it would be advisable for people with this placement to read that book. On a brighter note, there is so much energy to do good things here, that life will be full and happy, blessed as it is with the protection of the Creator. Direct dialogue with the Creator is possible with this placement.

Earth/Venus 2 in the 2nd House of Values: Earth/Venus 1 would have been concerned mainly for the comfort of their own families in this aspect of the House of Values, but Earth/Venus 2 Beings are much more active outside the home, and they have a larger family: a national, international, and universal one that they need to advocate for. Spiritual Tests in this arena call for proactive intervention to protect the innocent. All innocents. To do so may mean that the family of Earth/Venus 2 Beings, who are used to all of these people's attention, may have to become a little more independent so that mom or dad can work in the food bank or can lecture around the world about children's rights. This Spiritual Test calls for stepping outside of comfort zones to face areas that require attention. It may not be easy for the loving Earth/Venus people and they might have to come home once in awhile to curl into a ball, hug their kids, their dogs, and cats, and make everybody cookies. It is improbable that Earth/Venus 2 people will waste any money on needless knickknacks or home décor. They will, in all likelihood, be spending their extra cash on other families' needs, and they will encourage their children to giving away excess toys and clothes too.

Mercury in the 3rd House of Conscious Mind: Mercury Beings have few illusions about being easy to live with. They know that like the metal for which they are named, they tend to melt under the slightest heat and flow away. It is a wonder to them, really, that anyone would be willing to put up with them. When they love someone enough to realize that their mercurial ways hurt them and the "running away" will no longer cut it, they can be dedicated partners in the relationship. In order for a mercurial love to be steadfast, the love interest has to be ready to flow too, and the lifelong dance that ensues will be non-traditional, magical, fun, and vibrant.

LOVE ASPECT CHART 5

5	Sun 1
6	Moon 1
7	Earth/Venus 1
8	Mars
9	Neptune
10	Saturn
11	Uranus
12	Minerva
1	Sun 2
2	Moon 2
3	Earth/Venus 2
4	Mercury

Sun 1 in the 5th House of Love Aspect: When Sun Beings love, they love with all of their soul but there is always a separate part of themselves held in reserve for their individuality that speaks every bit as loudly. The partners of Sun 1 Beings will have to be very understanding indeed. They will need to be strong partners able to stand on their own, knowing they are loved, but not attached at the hip to the loved one. A certain amount of freedom is needed by Sun 1 Beings, but too much slack in the leash will allow them room to roam. The Sun Beings exude sexual energy. It's just the way they are. Sometimes they get caught up in someone else's attempts to snare them. Sun people separate love from sex, and unless they are with a partner that keeps life fresh and new and is interesting, diverse and valued, they may stray. If Sun Beings with this aspect fall deeply in love, they fall for the ones who don't bore them and who are strong enough to keep their own individualities. If they are committed to the relationship, these bright, shining, charming stars have the capability to love fully and stay home. Just break out the costumes.

Moon 1 in the 6th House of Physical Aspect: Moon Beings are generally softies. They like to mother everything, and recognize this tendency within themselves but with the charismatic and psychic Saturn behind this placement, the possibility of anyone using this to manipulate them comes to a dead stop. No lie, no deception, no subterfuge will escape the perception of these Moon Beings. They will likely be made of stern stuff and are very unlikely to mold their personalities to fit anyone else's ideal. They will be much more gregarious and assertive in their actions, and will have the confidence to stand up diplomatically for themselves and anyone else being trod upon. With the aspect of Saturn's dimensional thinking, these Moon Beings will be powerhouses of organization, mediation, and fundraising, and it's a fairly safe bet that they are the glue that holds their homes and work places together. The Spiritual Test for this placement is for the Moon Beings to enjoy learning Lifeforce lessons and to be pro-active in their strengths.

Earth/Venus 1 in the 7th House of Emotional Aspect: Earth and Venus energies are in perfect balance and surprisingly so are the

Uranus energies which sit behind the 7th House of Emotional Aspect. The Uranus part of this Earth/Venus nexus has a chance to break old patterns of disappointing people with broken promises here with the gift of finally caring so much about the possibility of hurting loved ones, that it becomes impossible to continue hurting them. These people finally grow up to recognize that the needs of loved ones take priority over the selfish need to repeat the pattern of testing and retesting for acceptance. The Earth/Venus people grow to understand that the secret to happiness is loving something or someone else more than themselves. However, in order for this all to work, they have to learn to love the faces in the mirror first.

Mars in the 8th House of Generation: The planet Mars generally deals out energy that may cause trouble, discord, and aggressive behavior but Minerva is there to balance the overabundance of machismo so Mars Beings have a chance to make the drama a *minor* drama. The reason it remains drama for these folks at all is that they will be tired from going to night school to learn astral projection, and how to manipulate the dreamstate aspects. Mars Beings have little patience for this kind of work and it makes them grouchy but it is necessary in their transformational development. Mars People are take charge, move into action kind of people. Since they first go to the physical as a way of handling things, Minervan teaching sets them asks a pretty hard task: it asks that they think first and observe, not react; and that they watch the natural progression of the consequences of how things flow. In Minervan dreamstate, the students are placed in situations requiring them to help other entities alter paths or decisions that could be disastrous or have negative outcomes. Mars Beings are all for jumping in and fixing things for them because it is really rough to watch others stumble and possibly put themselves at risk; but Mars' job is to watch a situation unwind. If it results in negative consequences, Mars Beings can stop the action before harm ensues, rewind the dream situation to the point where it went wrong, and lead their charges on another path; but that's it. They then have to observe what happens on the new path, which may turn out to be even more problematic for different reasons. Mars Beings' usual modus operandi is to find the path of least resistance, but that won't cut it now. The Spiritual Test for this aspect is patience, and methodical observation to help others along their spiritual paths. If you've drawn this card, Spirit is asking you to "go with the flow" and not react as you would normally react. Be patient, be observant and try to let those around you make their own mistakes. Don't try to intervene. The Spiritual Lesson is also to teach others not to always rely upon you but to rely upon themselves. Success will suit them and make them proud of themselves.

Neptune in the 9th House of Regeneration: The Planet Neptune has always had the reputation of being ego-centric. People with this placement have been working hard to overcome that aspect in order to make it this far in their spiritual transformation. In this aspect, Neptune Beings have a good helper, the Sun, which will be adding a lot of Lifeforce energy to balance the Loveforce energy that Neptunians normally have to deal with. This means that Neptune People finally have a chance to shine in the positive aspects of their traits. They will be working with Spirit now in a very real way to heal the waters of the Earth and to address the issues of pollution and protection of the planet's struggling Water creatures. These beings help to balance the Elemental aspect of Water with the other Elements. They will be working with higher souls to teach them about the Water Element and will be helping others to acclimate to Water. All higher aspect souls must be balanced eventually in all Elements, and Water is a toughie for some of them. If the higher aspect souls are Fire, for example, it is very difficult to convince them to douse their Fire with Water and learn about Water. Some just can't do it. Neptune people are extremely patient and well suited to teaching and helping others; they open up a venue for themselves to experience the soul satisfying aspect of watching others succeed. That smile when an obstacle is overcome and fears are put aside is worth all the effort, and the smile will be on Neptunes' faces too.

Saturn in the 10th House of Universal Lifeforce: When Saturn Beings reach this point, they have started to settle into comfortable dialogue with Spirit. They are actively working not only in dreamstate, but perhaps in waking dreams or visions during the day as well. Saturn People have always whizzed and whirled in a hundred mental directions. If they have arrived at this juncture, they probably now have this under control, and will be able to settle their lives down in general and start paying attention to what is important: their friends, their families, their chosen professions. People will remark that these Saturn people seem more relaxed and less stressed or hectic. This aspect will allow them to be more caring and more attentive to their mates, living in the moment for once, without needing to talk, or to be doing other things at the same time. Saturnians get to just "be" in this placement.

Uranus in the 11th House of Universal Loveforce: You are reaching a maturity where the drama and the chaos that you normally project or get involved in should be minimal, and you won't need it or want it in the future. It is important to the future journey of your soul that you direct your energies now to a broader scope. It is inherent in this placement that you actively pursue your social, political, or intellectual interests that affect not only yourself, but your planet. You are expected here to broadcast and use that great power to raise national and international consciousness to help save humanity from itself and to protect Mother Earth.

Minerva in the 12th House of Karma: We've all dreamed of being gypsy fortunetellers or trapeze artists who run off to the circus and live free lives. Minervan Beings are rather expected to do that sort of thing. If you have landed in this aspect, you have a lot of work to do in this lifetime to assure that your soul will continue on in the transformational journeys ahead. You need to pass three tests: Physical, Emotional, and Spiritual to achieve Fleur d'leis status for your soul to live past this lifetime. People think "Fleur d'leis" is a misspelling, when really it is an older spelling of the term, which means, "Flower of <u>Lifeforce</u>" in the stone or Pen'l Leina-Language. So a lot of work is needed to get and stay balanced, and it must be done. You may feel the need to have a spiritual journey, egged on by the many nights of dream teaching, or spiritual instruction during the day that lead you to DO SOMETHING. Spirit will never ask you to do something wrong. It may be as simple as stopping your car to give that street person $10.00, but you'd better listen, and not be afraid to act. That street person may be God in human form.

Sun 2 in the 1st House of Basis: Sun 2 energy gives spiritual direction straight from the Creator. Like Sun 1, these beings have the ability to work with energy and light to heal anything from a cell to a

Universe. However, unlike Sun 1, they are expected to be actively doing this work. Spirit is speaking to them and requesting their help. It is probable that they hear voices and those voices can be quite insistent about what help is needed. This help can take the form of lending a hand to a stranger or being awakened in the middle of the night by a bell ringing, a non-existent phone ringing, or knocking heard at the door when nobody is there. These are common signals to wake up and listen.

In order to facilitate hearing Spirit, it is advisable to wear metal to bed, in any non-negative, personally meaningful form; to work with a metal and stone pendulum; or keep a dream journal because the instruction manuals have been implanted and night school is in session. The Spiritual Tests on Earth toward transcendence are in full swing. Those with Sun 2 as their Birth Planet will probably have an irresistible urge to travel and may have to accept that they will be both teacher and student of the Universe throughout this lifetime.

Moon 2 in the 2nd House of Values: You are probably experiencing some fatigue because your higher self is going to "Love School." At this stage of spiritual transformation, it is expected by Spirit that you are also working universally on the physical plane in some direction to balance the energy equation of Loveforce energy, by writing, blogging, lecturing, teaching, and gathering positive and life affirming helpmates to do the work along the way. In this vein, it is important to remember that you cannot adopt or even help people into your life who are negative or energy draining, and not willing to do the necessary work to help themselves on the Earthly plane. That is definitely working backwards. Help those dependent upon you to break free of the need for your help. Traveling will probably be in the cards, and at some time in your life you will undertake a spiritual journey. Being open to Spirit's call is expected at this stage of your transformational journey, so try to stay balanced.

Earth/Venus 2 in the 3rd House of Conscious Mind: The children of these people will know, without a doubt, that they are loved. They are shown love in every way and their family life will be comfortable and generally happy. There will also be no doubt about who's boss. Mom's the boss. The female in this placement will broach no argument on that frontier. Any man married to a woman in this placement knows it too and accepts his fate. Conversely, the same would be true of a man in this placement. He will be a loving, somewhat strict father who is the head of the house.

The lesson of taking a personal stand and sticking with it will be learned early in a marital relationship. These people are very unlikely to allow abuse by another of their children or themselves. They are grounded in the reality of loving, caring relationships, and it is unlikely they will stay with someone who doesn't reciprocate that love. They will insist on being themselves and immediately try to improve everyone else around them. They can be exasperating, but they are deeply loved by their families, and will always champion the ones they love. The Spiritual Test, however, will be to let go, to relinquish control in an environment of trust and love. These beings must learn the lessons of waiting to be asked before giving an opinion or proposing a solution.

Mercury in the 4th House - Subconscious Mind: Mercury Beings have always had a sneaking suspicion that life would not be this hard if only they could get away from it all for awhile. The only problem is, the reason they want to get away is to keep from having to deal with responsibilities. It's not exactly their fault; they have responsibilities galore in the Soulforce Pool. Their higher-selves are helping to run things in the Universe, so when they get a chance to enjoy the physicality of Earth in this incarnation, they want to enjoy their freedom. Behind all the flakiness of their Earthly lives, however, there is a deep-seated responsibility to everything and everybody. They will rise to the cause of the right and just, and they will take care of their families, but anybody who is close to them can tell you that loving these Mercurial Beings is like being married to Peter Pan. How lucky Wendy would be, though, to keep the magic alive throughout her whole life!

If you've drawn this card, you are feeling trapped by the responsibilities of work and family and feel the need to get away from everything and everybody. You feel like you're being overworked, and it is difficult to get good rest. The Universe is demanding your attention because they need your help. You are tired because you are working with and for them in sleep phases, and you're starting to get worn out. Take heart! There is light at the end of this dream work phase, and things will settle down soon so that you can rest. You're doing important work that must be done.

PHYSICAL ASPECT CHART 6

6	Sun 1
7	Moon 1
8	Earth/Venus 1
9	Mars
10	Neptune
11	Saturn
12	Uranus
1	Minerva
2	Sun 2
3	Moon 2
4	Earth/Venus 2
5	Mercury

Sun 1 in the 6th House of Physical Aspect: These beautiful people will be blessed with good self-esteem and innate understanding of the blessedness of all things. People with this placement will love to be outdoors, perhaps gardening, or being close to nature. They will understand the subtle changes in the Earth and heavens. They often have everyone confiding everything to them, seeking their advice. These people are capable of sunny, positive, and life-affirming advice. They strive to help make others feel good about themselves and their decisions.

Moon 1 in the 7th House of Emotional Aspect: The energy of Uranus underlies this aspect and Uranus presents challenges. Moon people have financial difficulties because they are very generous and want beauty all around them. With this aspect, finances may get out of control. Moon Beings always center their lives on family, and because this is so, they strive for peace and comfort, but there may be discord instead. A Spiritual Test in this aspect is to learn the harder lessons from Lifeforce, which will only intensify and get worse if they are not addressed.

If you have drawn this card, some hard lessons may be coming down the pike, especially regarding finances. This placement is "what is happening now," so be forewarned. It is also not a time to spend frivolously, relax the rules, forego restrictions, or tolerate errant behavior in children, especially teens or pre-teens. Be extra vigilant, but don't assume that the problem is what appears to be evident. Listen to all sides and be prepared to be a strong supportive parent.

Earth/Venus 1 in the 8th House of Generation: Earth Element people are grounded, rooted, and like to be close to the Earth. Their deep connection to the Earth is something that the other signs crave and rarely feel. . They are tied to Mother Earth and their mothers will be important.

These Earth/Venus1 beings tend to observe the situation and process before they decide what is going on. They form their own opinions. They are sensual, tactile, and love to eat. You'll often hear them say they need "comfort food." They have to watch a tendency to over-eat and suffer health problems as a result of that.

They have a tendency, when disconnected from Earth's energy, to experience depression or ennui. When that happens, they need to go outside and lie in the grass and soak up Sun and Earth energy. Earth Element people are loving individuals and are generally loved by their families. They have a great sense of humor and their laughs and giggles are infectious.

They are realistic and will do what it takes to get the job done, and then they want to go play outside. They were the kids at school who chanted, "Is it time for recess yet? Is it time for recess yet?" The Spiritual Test of Earth/Venus 1 people in the House of Generation is to stand up for the underdog and not condone abuse. Their Venus lesson is to love and teach others to love responsibly.

Mars in the 9th House of Regeneration: If Mars Beings have reached this point, they are well on their way to finding love, peace, and happiness on the Earthly plane and deep spiritual fulfillment when they incarnate again. For now, Mars Beings can just enjoy being happy. They are finally ready to start looking for partners, and if they've found their soulmates, Mars can finally relax and enjoy that miracle.

Neptune in the 10th House of Universal Lifeforce: Dolphins and whales sing healing to the Universe. From under the seas they sit in two dimensions and work tirelessly to heal Loveforce energy for planet Earth, for the spiritual realms, and for every transcended being on the planet Earth. Neptune Beings will forever be tied to water bodies and the Water Element, for they sense their responsibility to keep things flowing. In this House of Universal Lifeforce, they are working on a very big picture indeed: keeping the balance of power between planet Earth and the other planets and dimensions in our solar system in harmonious order. People who have this aspect have one more task to accomplish before transcending to join the Soulforce Pool. They must lose their ego. I used to read this all the time in astrology books and it always frustrated me. What does that mean? It means you can't trick Spirit into noticing how humble you are or how selflessly you are living your life in service to others. You are doing everything you're supposed to in order to earn your soul, but it is as if you are saying, "Just look at how good I've been and what I've accomplished." There is the problem. The fact that you are still calling attention to yourself in hope of being rewarded is still ego. In this lifetime, the lesson must be to offer yourself in pure love for the benefit of teaching and helping others to understand Loveforce, and to take joy in their joy and success without even a hint of wanting something back. You will have help. Spirit will place many opportunities in your path to practice "not calling attention to yourself." When you finally "get it," you'll be an Angel on Earth.

Saturn in the 11th House of Universal Loveforce: Saturn Beings have worked very hard to make it this far. The Universal House of Loveforce is the final testing aspect in this incarnation. Saturn people have always enjoyed psychic and intuitive skills, but if this aspect shows up, they have learned to fine-tune their talents. Saturn people's thought patterns work in rings around the crux of the matter, circular arguments that spin and whiz and work so quickly that they can view a problem and come up with many solutions before people even realize there is a problem. They think dimensionally and definitely outside the box. They've always had a view slightly askew, and when it was based around ego, it generally acted as a self-serving instrument. However, in this aspect, any negativity in this regard is transcended.

These beings have managed to calm the chaos and quiet a busy and distracted mind to work for the good of the whole Universe. At this point they have wrestled with that overwhelming sense of self-importance to get in line with the spiritual work they must do. They've learned to sift the wheat from the chaff in their perceptions and have learned to prioritize. The transformational finish here is to lose any residual ego that wants reward for good behavior. Anything done in Universal Loveforce has to be done as both teacher and student and in loving sacrifice to the greater good. At the point where Saturn Beings feel joy in someone else's accomplishments and success, when they deeply experience the joy of heartfelt wonder for another, they are on the right path for oneness in the Soulforce Pool.

Uranus in the 12th House of Karma: Uranus needs to be congratulated, because they have finally arrived at the starting line after many probable lifetimes of struggle to get here. Uranians are expected to have learned their karmic lessons and calmed down. In past incarnations, these beings have been sorely tested. Now they are expected to have learned the three cosmic laws of responsibility: we own our own souls; we are responsible for our own souls; and we alone must take the consequences for our decisions and actions. Bravo! They have "endeavored to persevere" and have won a place with Spirit to help the Creator with the matrix of the Universe, to balance energies between planets, to counsel or guide warrior spirits. If they are here, they have been accepted among the ranks of the Creator's elite guard, the Walkers, and have been sent back in an incarnation to aid Spirit in some way.

Minerva in the 1st House of Basis: All psychic abilities and ability to work with Spirit in the dreamstate will be enhanced in this aspect. You won't have vague whisperings or half feelings that you are gifted as something more in this life. You will know it without any question. If you stay balanced, you will be doing Spirit's work on Earth, and it will be something akin to being an Angel on Earth; allow yourself to trust your dreams, and follow the guidance you are being given. If you are happy, balanced, and take care of your body, exercise, and eat right, a whole new world is about to open up for you. You will be receiving communication from Spirit in your dreams, and the nightly teaching will open up psychic and intuitive abilities far more clearly than you have ever previously experienced. However, if you are unhappy and not balanced, you will be missing a wonderful opportunity. A key to staying balanced is to make sure you get more rest than usual. Your higher-self will be going to night school, and upon graduation, you will have earned mental clarity and a rich spiritual connection. If you don't allow for the extra hours of night school, you'll be too weary to stay balanced. Catch 22.

Sun 2 in the 2nd House of Values: These people are not easy people to live with or understand. There may be almost constant discord between partners, but make-up sex later will always be dynamic. The higher being Sun 2 in the House of Values can be god-like tyrants, but they should not be allowed to get away with acting like that. This is the key to understanding life with Sun 2 Beings in the House of Values: if someone who is supposed to be an equal power and partner attempts to make unilateral decisions, ANY unilateral decisions, there will be discord. Period. It isn't really a matter of who wields the final say. It will be more about the audacity of somebody else daring to try to exert their will over Sun's 2 will. Wants, needs, and decisions must be discussed and agreed upon in advance regarding money issues, décor, and child rearing. It's important to be aware of the point when it's time to find common ground. The ability to compromise is definitely a Spiritual Test in this aspect.

It must be remembered that neither partner should take this test of wills personally. If the partners will listen and state their own cases quietly, there is more harmony. Sun Beings crave harmony and balance, but they tend to constantly instigate things that cause disharmony in their surroundings. In the final analysis, their mates are part of their surroundings. Sun Beings really don't want permanent discord with them either. Their Spiritual Test is to learn to value the opinions and feelings of others by practicing complete silence and learn to listen without feeling the need to fix everything and everybody. Let the other person have their way sometimes. Sun Beings must learn to pick battles that are important and not fight every battle.

Moon 2 in the 3rd House of the Conscious Mind: Moon 2 people have a view askew from most people; they give a whole new meaning to the phrase "going with the flow." They are under the influence primarily of Venus, the quintessential mature love. These people have earned a place beside Diana to help souls move from incarnation to incarnation and figure out their Lifescript plans for the next life. A Venuvian's concept of love is pure and envisions what mankind can aspire to, but never fully reach. They have no self-concept, no giant egos, or problems with esteem. They are selfless beings. They are complete within themselves, and if you are fortunate enough to have drawn this aspect, it is a spiritual message that you are on the right track to losing ego and becoming a complete, mature spiritual being. What others see is you: confident, with no pretenses, and no need to impress. This means you are balancing yourself admirably male to female and your self-image is true to the mark. You are perfectly ok with you, and certainly you are ok with Spirit.

Earth/Venus 2 in the 4th House of the Subconscious Mind: These Earth and Venus Beings aren't very comfortable with hiding anything. Because Earth and Venus are primarily Loveforce energies, and one test of love is truthfulness and disclosure, hiding things in Loveforce is not second nature, but it is a necessary Lifeforce lesson for all of mankind. Love is kind, but to not keep some things hidden would not be kind. Brutal honesty is just that...brutal, and it is unnecessary.

If you have drawn the card for Earth/Venus 2 in the 4th House, the test for this higher spiritual aspect will be to consider the consequences of telling the truth for others, indulging in the basic selfish need to have everything on the table, regardless of whom it hurts. Truth can sometimes be held in reserve until the time is right to speak it. Versions of truth, which cause less pain, can be told if something must be said. You can be truthful without causing pain. Diplomacy is the lesson here.

Mercury in the 5th House of Love Aspect: These individuals are so charming, loving and fun that they will attract mates like bees to honey. They can be good friends, and are generally very interested in sex. They just don't like commitment or responsibilities, and loving someone is a big bunch of both. In all probability, they will spend a great deal of time playing the field or having one-night stands before they fall head over heels in love with their soul mate. Once they commit to a relationship, they are committed 100%, and they will be faithful as long as their partner is. If the partner is unfaithful, however, the marriage is over. Being faithful is hard for them, and if Mercury Beings have to work at it, their partners are expected to work at it too. It is as probable that the partner will be of the same sex as of opposite sex.

If the partners are the opposite sex and there are children, Mercury Beings will be unorthodox parents who will only partially participate in raising them. The children will be toys to play with and Mercurians will give them 100% of their attention and love when they are around; however, they may not be around consistently. Mercury Beings are social and busy in general and will have a need to travel and have quality time alone. The partners of Mercury Beings will need to understand that a certain amount of freedom and distance from responsibility is necessary for their mates' happiness.

Mercury Beings will always provide well for their families, and will love to cook but won't clean up the mess. They will struggle with being the adult partners with regard to day-to-day responsibilities unless those responsibilities involve fun or adventure. The Mercury Beings flee from drudgery, and would rather pay for domestic help than pick up a vacuum, but if people are needed to fly a kite with, the Mercury Beings are the ones who will joyfully spend hours teaching everybody to make one from scratch.

If Mercury Beings don't marry, they will probably travel. They will have a huge bank of friends who are like family and they will never settle down for long with any of them. Their friends will love them for life, but will always be wondering where they are. Suddenly, their Mercurial friends will be on their doorstep and it will be as if there was never any gap in time since they last saw each other. Mercury Beings are life-long friends and a really good friends. If there is a commitment given, it will be special indeed, and it will always be honored.

EMOTIONAL ASPECT CHART 7

7   Sun 1
8   Moon 1
9   Earth/Venus 1
10 Mars
11 Neptune
12 Saturn
1   Uranus
2   Minerva
3   Sun 2
4   Moon 2
5   Earth/Venus 2
6   Mercury

Sun 1 in the 7th House of Emotional Aspect: Sun 1 energy is stronger than Uranus, the background power here, so it can help someone with this aspect to overcome obstacles. Uranus energy influences the Sun 1 Beings to make promises they can't possibly keep so that their loved ones are either continuously disappointed, or find it hard to believe in or count on anything their Uranus-influenced friends or loved ones do or say. Nothing can be more confusing or discouraging than this. A Sun 1 heart wants very badly to give, and would be very willing to give, just about anything in its power to please friends and families. Sun energy here tests these people to "make no promises, break no promises" in this aspect, and when they learn to stop promising things that can't be delivered, they will break a pattern of many lifetimes, and people will start trusting them again. Emotionally, it's important to remember that the underlying Uranus energy is childlike in wanting to please everyone for acceptance. The Spiritual Test will be to recognize that although they may want to please, they cannot please everybody. What they can do is try to please their Spiritual Guide and in doing so, life will be sunnier and happier.

Moon 1 in the 8th House of Generation: These dreamy individuals understand that the work they are doing in Dreamtime or in astral states is very important. They have accepted that they have a job to do for the Universe. Minerva is the energy behind this placement in the 8th House of "What is," and while this may not be what we want it to be, it truly is where we are on our transformational path. If Moon Beings are balanced Elementally, they are right where they should be.

Although we are primarily two main Elements, we experience living in and receiving teachings from all of them throughout the course of our spiritual lives. Transitioning from one to another isn't always easy. Sometimes our spiritual bodies resist an unknown Element. If you are primarily a Fire Element, trying to accommodate your personality to Water, for example, you face no small task. Fire doesn't like Water. It smothers it, and a really good water dousing will put it out entirely.

The result of living in and studying the differences between the Elements will make us more complete. We cannot be "fully cooked" until we have experienced them all. Spirit's test in this aspect is to learn to "go with the flow" of the current Elemental teacher, and to try to relax and learn from the Element. Our reward? We can take that energy from Fire and Water and make steam, and then ride that steam into the sky to dance with the Air Elementals. We will all learn the dances; it just takes time and several lifetimes of practice.

Earth/Venus 1 in the 9th House of Regeneration: Because this individual is blessed with the possibility of perfect balance of Lifeforce and Loveforce energy as well as a blessed life, an Earth/Venus 2 placement is expected to give back. Spirit will test this individual by asking for help and healing. If the individual stays balanced, they can hear cries for help from the Godhead and/or Soulforce Pool, and they must be prepared to help. They must answer the literal spiritual phone or doorbell when it rings at all hours of the night or day and listen for instructions. Say," I hear you, what can I do for YOU?" three times and then be amazed when they answer.

Mars in the 10th House of Universal Lifeforce: By the time Mars warriors reach this placement of Universal Lifeforce, they are expected to have battled their demons, forgiven themselves for being alive, and moved on towards working hard on that love thing. If they aren't there yet, they aren't listening to the Angels whispering in their ears constantly guiding them; *and they have great guides*, the Sun/Creator, and the Moon/Diana. Lots of transformational work has been done for their souls to get this far, and Spirit is going to be there with these Mars Beings every step of the way. If people drawing this card don't see themselves as warriors, they will have a hard time explaining their dreams. Their higher souls fight a good fight all night long, and it isn't inconceivable that the fatigue felt is battle fatigue. People with this placement have set themselves the task in this lifetime to defend and protect in one dimension or another. That is what they are doing and what they must continue to do.

Neptune in the 11th House of Universal Loveforce: Life will be much richer and fuller than you've ever experienced in any other lifetime, and you have already earned a place in the Soulforce Pool by virtue of making it this far. You have already passed the test of flowing Universal Lifeforce, which wasn't at all easy because you are weighed so very heavily in Loveforce in this aspect. You are a powerful Universal Being indeed! Enjoy a peace you've never felt before. Enjoy that sigh of relief and take a deep breath of contentment. This lifetime will be a joy, likely spent in service to others. The satisfaction you'll experience enjoying their accomplishments will be monumental in your life and in theirs. It is probable that you will also feel a need to protect in this lifetime, and Spirit is hopeful that you will be proactive for the creatures of the Sea and the health of Earth's waters. However, even if you are not actively advocating for the Water Element on the Planet, you are doing the work you need to do in your sleep. Enjoy this sweet life that you've worked so hard to earn!

Saturn in the 12th House of Karma: Bravo! For Saturn Beings to reach the House of Karma, they had to overcome very much. They had to fine-tune their psychic and intuitive skills to a master level. They had to calm all the voices in their heads and ask for and receive one guide, one voice. In doing so, they have found a peace and happiness they have been searching for for a multitude of lifetimes. It is very, very rare for Saturn Beings to make it this far. Usually the cacophony of stimulus and the constant barrage of outside forces and demands causes Saturn Beings to seek peace by stilling the chaos and shutting it all down. This sign is the mark of a truly evolved soul who has worked hard to get here and as a reward, Spirit asks only for occasional help so that Saturns can enjoy their Earthly lives, their friends and families and a peace they have never known before.

Uranus in the 1st House of Basis: The Sun (Godhead) is here to help guide and calm these lucky Uranus Beings. Life will make more sense and will be less dramatic if they can just train themselves to trust their gut instincts because spiritual help will stream from the navel chakra in this instance. A sick tummy or a queasy, uneasy feeling is a real clue to stop, regroup, and think about what is going on and how to proceed in the higher path.

If you have pulled this card, trust your gut feelings. Run when your instinct says run, or fight for what is right when your tummy twists up.

The Sun's influence here is a test of your mettle: can you handle the situation like an adult would and should? Don't accept bad manners or poor demeaning behavior without speaking out. It can be done without punching an offender in the nose because your stomach will warn you and the Godhead is there telling you how to proceed. If you stay balanced, you can get the very best benefit of this placement.

If you are unbalanced, ignoring your gut feelings may result in an ulcer or acid indigestion. If this is a problem, put away the antacids and practice your speech (the one where you're sticking up for yourself or others or the one in which you have figured out a solution to a problem and you need someone to listen). Make a game plan for how you can change the dynamics of a situation that is eating you up. You have BIG help cheering you on and giving you insight.

Minerva in the 2nd House of Values: Friends and family know they can trust these people and can confide in them because they sense inherently that everything that is confided is understood. If they only knew! Not only can Minervans understand them, they feel what they feel, see what they see, and experience both their pleasure and their pain. Minervan Beings also know what people are going to say before it is said, so there is no point whatsoever in attempting to lie to them. They can detect a lie, an exaggeration, or dramatization effortlessly so don't even bother trying to deceive them. Lies will not be forgiven. Minervan Beings hate liars. Marriage to a Minervan will require utter honesty, and that must never be forgotten. They will have difficulty not reacting to things they perceive psychically. They are excellent mediators and can always calm troubled waters. They stay tapped in to the people they love and can tell when their loved ones are stressed or in trouble. Minervans' dream lives and spiritual work keep them rather tired, and may make them a little irritated during the day, but even at their worst, they are still loving and caring.

The Minervans aren't particularly materialistic, and their homes are usually simple and functional as opposed to cluttered or cozy. When they make cookies, they'll probably make twelve dozen at a time to freeze for later. Because Minervan people are so pleasant and understanding, don't think for a moment that they can be taken for granted or exploited in any way. They are street smart and experienced beyond imagination in the way of the world because they walk a much higher road than most and they can walk in anyone's shoes.

Sun 2 in the 3rd House of the Conscious Mind: The face of the Sun is the face of the Creator. We cannot gaze into the Sun without becoming blind. Likewise, we cannot gaze into the true face of the Creator/God/Sun. The House of the Conscious Mind, is supposed to reveal that which is shown. The intellect and consciousness of the Creator, the protector, the Father of us all, is encased in a lonely visage that remains hidden from us. But the Creator was born of himself in the House of Basis, and he had a plan. He would materialize and share the best parts of himself with a lovely feminine mate, Diana, created out of his ideals for the best partner and the essential mother. The combination of their energies would create life on Earth as well as other dimensions and other planets. The Creator would split his energies and share the best parts of himself with another, the one many call God. This ideal God, the benevolent and loving God in a visage that could be seen and heard, would keep the appearance of man and would love humankind above all of his creations.

This concept of Father, Son and Holy Ghost, this triad of the Creator, has always confused us. We all know on some level that the Creator's form cannot be seen, but we do also know that the Sun is an energy that lives in us all. We are a part of the Godhead. We are not individual Beings. We are Energy Beings given a body in order to enjoy the physicality of Earthly life. In truth, our energy melds into all other energies in a dimensional extension of the Soulforce Pool. While we are seemingly independent and autonomous forms, we are actually a group form, beautiful Beings of light and color. That is the soul, and how Spirit sees us. So, what most of us see is not *really* what we are either.

Because this aspect is so complicated, life is always complicated for the individuals with this aspect. These people have a unique perspective on understanding that what we see is not all that there is. There is a measure of perception that extends to accepting the actual materialization of Spirit versus what appears to be seen. They understand bone deep isolation. Like Sun 1 in the 3rd House, not only do they understand the duality of our forms, that we are both male and female energies, but they understand an androgynous quality as well within themselves and in their partners. Their capacity for love, and caring, and nurturing knows no boundaries, and makes no judgement on what is 'acceptable."

Moon 2 in the 4th House of the Subconscious Mind: Moon 2 is advanced training from the Moon 1 aspect of simply learning reciprocity and self-value. It goes beyond learning to deal with frustration and anger to enabling the Moon 2 people to do something about what is causing that anger. Think of this placement as being a mother tigers protecting her kits. Anybody daring to get between them will be dinner. We can't literally tear someone apart for abusing our children, or any innocents, but we can certainly stand up for them, believe in them, and help them learn to address any wrongs being done to them. The toughest part of being parents is giving our children a firm sense of their own power and responsibility for righting their own wrongs. Parents and protectors must also recognize that point when consequences are too severe for a minor infractions. Moon 2 Beings must be prepared to step-in and lend a guiding hand. Not all of us are mothers or fathers, but we being asked to help guide innocents away from abuse, to protect them, and to help them to defend themselves, with a little help from their friends if necessary.

Earth/Venus 2 in the 5th House of Love Aspect: Sometimes we have to make hard choices. We have to give up something we want for something someone else wants or needs. The people who are under this aspect know that already, and they have already sacrificed a great deal for their families, their fellows, for the Universe, and for the Spiritual Pool. Sometimes the Universe recognizes a job well done and just allows some freedom to sigh and enjoy the experience of living in a solid body in an Earthly plane. Physicality is a gift, enjoying life in general and family life in particular may be experiences some spiritual beings have never had. Having tensile touch, and just being able to relish the joy of eating and making joyful noises; laughing with their children, playing with the dog and having family dinners with their loved ones, is something treasured by Spirit. This is one of those incidences, because if anyone ever deserved to just enjoy love and life, these people have certainly earned the right to "just be." If you have drawn this card, know that you are loved and appreciated, and Spirit wants the very best for you for a job well done. Blessings to you.

Mercury in the 6th House of Physical Aspect: Mercury Beings are beautiful people. They are larger than life, attractive, and fun to be around; at least that is true in the minds of the Mercurians. This is probably not the way other people actually see them. Mercury Beings have pretty big egos, and they know they are attractive, but most people don't appreciate arrogance and conceit and Mercury Beings can surely appear that way. To call them conceited and arrogant isn't really fair to the Mercury Beings, however. They are naturally skilled, lucky in business, and have a sixth sense for what will be successful and profitable and what won't.

They are exuberant, enthusiastic, and gung-ho to bring great ideas to fruition, but they can't be counted on if things start to go south, and that is their karmic struggle. They are essentially rather flaky. It's not that they don't want to finish the project; they feel like they've already given their best ideas and energy to it, and "If it's "going too slow, it's not going to go." So Mercury people go off onto something else that might actually get done. If you can ride their rollercoaster, the projects you work on with Mercury people will probably shine and they will be successful. Mercury Beings will work hard on something they believe in with people who will work as hard as they. However, drop the ball and they will too; they'll move on to something else.

GENERATION CHART 8

8 Sun 1
9 Moon 1
10 Earth/Venus 1
11 Mars
12 Neptune
1 Saturn
2 Uranus
3 Minerva
4 Sun 2
5 Moon 2
6 Earth/Venus 2
7 Mercury

Sun 1 in the 8th House of Generation: These people are struggling with lots of issues: responsibility, happiness, faith, day-to-day monotony, and feeling out of step with everything. Having to be the "responsible one" is oppressive to them. Minerva influences this placement, and Minerva has an itchy travel bug. At the same time that these Sun people are trying to be a good employers, employees, husbands, wives, or parents, they are also wanting and needing to run away from it all. They may deliberately sabotage their own success or advancement in a job if it is too demanding or oppressive. These Sun Beings are not necessarily irresponsible or uncaring, but they can be.

On a deep, inherent level, they feel that they must have a great deal of alone time to regroup and recoup in their busy minds. Someone trying to look over their shoulder or micromanage any of their efforts will make the Sun Beings extremely unhappy and twitchy. Unreasonable deadlines and honey-do lists will go astray.

Sometimes, the family will just have to understand that these individuals have to get completely away from everyday everything and everybody for a few days. They need breathing room and may have a need for adventure. They may have a completely separate set of friends that they enjoy a certain amount of freedom with. The partners or families of these Sun people should expect secret pals or societies. The Sun Beings will come back ready to face their responsibilities again, but must be allowed some occasional freedom to roam and misbehave.

These individuals are often spacey and distracted and have a tendency to daydream. They are dealing with a lot of unanswered questions that only they can answer. They will have to clean their Spiritual, Emotional, and Physical houses in this lifetime, and that will require parting with negative, clinging friends and relatives, eliminating as many material goods as possible, and addressing that need for private physical space and understanding.

Moon 1 in the 9th House of Regeneration: The Godhead in the House of Regeneration brings spiritual protection and guidance throughout these Moon Beings' lives as they are being trained to join Spirit in the Soulforce Pool at the end of this natural lifetime. In this lifetime, the Moon Beings need to accept that they are doing Spirit's work on Earth, whether or not others may understand.

These people will be working with others to teach the love aspect, heal the Loveforce balance, and promote love in all things. Their highest teaching is living love, the most shining example of these people living their faith without the need to be recognized or rewarded for it. They will understand true humility, and indeed may be Angels returned to Earth after having transcended, on some task from Spirit. They will feel white light spiritual presence, and hear the voice of Spirit provided they stay balanced male to female and elementally. The Sun is the revitalizing force for these individuals and the Sun will channel the necessary energy and instruction to Moon Beings in order that they may do what is asked.

Earth/Venus 1 in the 10th House of Universal Lifeforce: Earth is the training ground for spiritual trial, and Venus is the aspect of the test of love in this lifetime. This is the perfect placement to study universal love and to learn to understand the spiritual connection. In order to be well balanced, the Earth/Venus Being will have to learn to operate with Lifeforce energy and practice saying "no" when instincts say to say no. A test may be tough love at work or at home, and the ability to love the self enough to stand up when it counts.

Mars in the 11th House of Universal Loveforce: When warriors have to do battle, it wears on the heart, hardening it and making it difficult to love without also dealing with the possibility of loss. Warriors tend to love in spite of themselves. They love their fellow soldiers, and they love their families. They do the awful things they have to do to protect and defend their brothers and sisters in arms and to keep their families safe. Because Spirit understands that warrior work is emotionally pricey, they are there with the big guns. Major powers of Earth 2, Venus 2, and Moon 2 energies stand at warriors' shoulders. The feminine energies will help to soothe the pain and heal individuals; helping them to look at the world with more loving eyes.

If those who draw this card don't see themselves as warriors, it is understandable, but in all transformational paths, we have all been warriors in many lifetimes. Much of the work being done in this position is being done as the higher-self. It is conceivable that if these Beings feel like they never gets any rest and are always tired, it is because Spirit keeps them busy at night. The other part of this placement is that these people will be called upon not only to love, but also to know when to use tough love. However, they need to be able to discern when to be tough, and when not to react and to trust their loved ones and just listen.

Neptune in the 12th House of Karma: For Neptune Beings to reach the House of Karma, they have had to learn many lessons. The biggest one was to learn to love themselves unconditionally before they could love another. They have learned to lose the egos that chained them to behaviors that only made them and those around them unhappy. That is no small task, but they have passed these tests.

They have learned to help with all aspects of the Water Elements, and are working to both heal the planet, and help their fellow Water Beings. They have even passed the tests of the Elementals. They have had to deal with being all six Elements by now, and that makes them much better rounded. As with all signs in the House of Karma, they can relax and enjoy their Earthly lives, living under the three-fold blessing of instant karma. They are so amazed and thrilled to be in this aspect in their higher selves, it is very unlikely they will have to face the three-fold retribution part of harming a pure heart. On the Earthly side of this, these Water babies will have a hard time not being on the beach or immersed in water to dance their joy! Of all the signs that may travel to follow the Sun, it is likely that many of them have this aspect in their charts. Spirit wants them to enjoy their accomplishments and blesses, and thanks them.

Saturn in the 1st House of Basis: The motivating energy in the House of Basis is the Sun, and that is fortunate for gregarious Saturn Beings. These folks are naturally light and bright, and adding the Sun's energy just makes them more so. It also helps to guide what might be a "chatterbox" to being someone with something to say, and someone to whom the masses will listen. The reason is that Lifeforce and Loveforce are amplified here, but balanced well, so that with just the smallest amount of effort, these individuals may stay eternally balanced. As such, these beings are happy, well adjusted, and larger than life. They will walk into a room, and all eyes will follow them, whether they are ten or ninety, have a model's body, or have put on a few extra pounds.

If you have pulled this card, you have received a blessing. The Sun is lending his energy to the gregarious, happy part of you. Whatever you are trying to say will be heard, and whatever you are trying to do, people will want to help you to do it. If you are attempting to raise consciousness, this is the perfect placement for it if you are balanced. If you are unbalanced (and you will know this by either being basically happy and at peace, or not), a different energy is at work here. First off, what did you do to yourself to get to this point? You had to go out of your way to unhinge what has been the Universe's gift of perfect balance. All the gifts given here (your dynamic personality, the ability to sway the masses, and influence others) may work against you in an imbalanced state. To fix this, all you have to do is stop the negative thinking and speaking, and stop whatever you are doing to pollute your body. It won't take long to go in the right direction and for the positive and life-affirming forces to return to you. Be strong, avoid the junk food aisles, and eat your fruits and vegetables.

Uranus in the 2nd House of Values: Uranus Beings are, in many ways, very young souls, and as a result, they can be materially single minded and stubborn in their drive to get what they want when they want it, and determined to get their way. If Uranians are single, then they may find themselves with ridiculous toys, and in financial difficulty due to self-indulgence, but if Uranus Beings are mated, an "I deserve this" attitude will not be appreciated by their partners. Uranus Beings have a tendency to promise children expensive things they can't afford or which are not age appropriate, and they must learn not to make pie in the sky promises to their mates or their children that will put the family in financial difficulty or are simply not possible. "Make no promises, break no promises" needs to be their battle cry.

he Transformational Test here is for Uranus people to learn to weigh the consequences of selfish and unilateral decisions against something that is more important, like reality, and relationships. The Spiritual Tests for Uranus Beings in the 2nd House of Values will be more on a material level of learning to live within their means and to practice self-denial for the greater good of someone else.

Minerva in the 3rd House of Conscious Mind: The face these Minervans show to others is that of an understanding, patient, and competent mediator for everybody else's dysfunctions. People tell Minervans everything, and because Minervans are good listeners and honestly do not appear to outwardly judge; they are often abused listeners. The people who control this abuse are obviously the Minervans themselves, but they've experienced enough of life in the shoes of the distracted and dysfunctional that they are almost immune to being shocked or dismayed over average people's capacity to misunderstand, misinterpret, and miscommunicate almost everything. Somebody has to straighten these poor souls out without letting on that they are being manipulated into helping themselves out of the holes they themselves may have dug. Being a personal savior to the dysfunctional masses begins to wear thin after a while. The test of this placement is to rein in the tendency to try to save people. Hole up and make yourself unavailable for a time so that the energies you are expending so generously can be recharged. After a period of rest, you can come back renewed, but if the same scenario threatens to play itself out again with the clueless, withdraw and do let it be known, that the advice you gave them before hasn't changed, and you trust that they will work it out. Quit spinning your wheels with the lost and hopeless.

Sun 2 in the 4th House of the Subconscious Mind: When we were children, we probably all fought taking naps. As a working adult, I often reminisce about naps in the sunshine, and wish someone would make me take a nap now. Curiously enough, these Sun 2 people are being given the task of sleeping and napping by Spirit in order to balance aggressive tendencies. Sun 2 energies in this placement have warrior Mars as the underlying Planetary influence. In order for the male dominated influences of Sun 2 and Mars to be balanced, Moon and Venus energy intervene, and make these people go to night school to balance the Loveforce energy that is unbalanced from this equation and combination. They must be sure to get at least ten hours rest at night, and grab quick naps during the day if they can. Even closing their eyes for ten minutes, and practicing deep breathing will help to calm troubled and turbulent seas. If they don't get enough rest (yes, I said ten hours!), they will be grouchy and aggressive, and that will just add to the problem that the Universe is helping them work out. Many people with this combination choose not to be married and play the field much longer than is healthy because they feel like they can't function fully and manage the day to day. The Spiritual Test for this problem is to sleep, and go to school. Dream work and dream teaching is vital to the success of balancing Loveforce energy so these people may move on in the transformational journeys ahead.

Moon 2 in the 5th House of Love Aspect: Venus is the power sitting behind Moon 2, and Venus has rather an alien view of things. Their approach to problems and their reaction to the emotional involvement of mates and children is very often a step off from what their families and friends are expecting and needing. Venus Beings are fully transcended, and they are the masters of "wait and see" and "don't worry, it will all work out in the end." The majority of the time it will, but that doesn't comfort or resolve teenage angst. Moon 2 people will just smile and pat them on the head when there may be underlying issues that truly need deeper investigation and a more motherly or fatherly approach. Pizza needs to be ordered, or cookies need to be baked and tea needs to be poured in order to calm the waters. Moon 2 people in this house are beginning to get a clue about these things, but sometimes they are slow enough on the uptake that teens especially may act out. Moon Beings can be pretty strict but they aren't always understanding; this occurs not because they don't want to understand but because they are genuinely clueless as to what the fuss is all about. The Spiritual Test for this aspect is to really try to look beyond the immediately obvious with a different perspective. Whether or not the Moon 2 Being completely understands, sometimes all it takes is reassurance, a big hug and being the people who listen and care. Tea and sympathy and cookies or pizza can't hurt.

Earth/Venus 2 in the 6th House of Physical Aspect: The people who fall under this aspect have no clue how wonderful they are. They are some of the few of us who have lost Earthly ego: they have trusted their higher-powers, guides, or Spirit and "let go, and let God." They can take pleasure in the pleasure of someone else, and feel great joy for the accomplishments of another. As to how they perceive themselves, they don't care. They are neither traditionally male nor female. They don't fit into nice categories of body types or current trendy dress styles. They have a style all their own, and a charm all their own. It doesn't really matter to them if they wear jeans to a dress ball. Their confidence and splendor shines through from the core of their being, and reflects in the understanding in their eyes, and their countenance of being. If they do go to that ball in jeans, one look into their eyes will guarantee that the person dancing with them won't care what they are wearing either.

Mercury in the 7th House of Emotional Aspect: Mercury Beings have their act together more than people think. The problem is that their priorities aren't what anybody else considers a priority; it is the stuff of dreams, dreamwork, daydreams, and planning for the future accomplishment of those dreams. Mercury Beings have that handled. When it comes to harder interactions, like courting friends or lovers, or smoozing with the boss or doing good coffee with fellow employees, they often miss the point of why that is important. If loved ones are patient, and allow the space for the Mercury Beings to think about what it is they really want to do, life flows smoother. Life with a Mercurian is a series of comings and goings, and confusion. The people around these people are confused too. They pick up on the Mercury Beings' conflicting need to go, and their need to stay, and often get hurt because Mercurians will choose to go more often than stay. The "Oh, stick around, don't go" plea will send them running for sure. They can't mind you. They can't be held in check with demands or ultimatums. Think of these Mercurians like cats. Turn your back and appear disinterested in what they do, while keeping yourself busy doing something interesting or mysterious or mischievous, and they'll serpentine through the room just to watch you. They will want to stick around, and play too.

REGENERATION CHART 9

9	Sun 1
10	Moon 1
11	Earth/Venus 1
12	Mars
1	Neptune
2	Saturn
3	Uranus
4	Minerva
5	Sun 2
6	Moon 2
7	Earth/Venus 2
8	Mercury

Sun 1 in the 9th House of Regeneration: People with this placement are being given Spiritual protection and guidance throughout their lives and are being trained to join Spirit in the Soulforce Pool. The gift is a blessing if the individuals will act; in whatever fashion they may, upon the direction they are given. Their work can be done quietly and alone with a help of a few of friends of like mind, even if the friends are rocks, animals or planets. They are doing Spirit's work on Earth and may have to accept that others may not understand this. The Sun is the revitalizing force for this individual and will channel the necessary energy and instruction to do what is asked. Prepare to listen.

Moon 1 in the 10th House of Universal Lifeforce: Let's look around the warm, eclectic home that we have created. Is there a corner for beads, or model planes or things stored in boxes under the bed for easy access? To be whole people, we have to have a creative side. Any creative endeavor that people have spent lifetimes perfecting is art. Creative endeavors serve spiritually to help balance the Universe. Sometimes the best help we can give Spirit is to finally work on the model airplane sitting in the closet, and daydream while we do it. What can be imagined can be created. What is envisioned as healed and whole, and beautiful can be made manifest. From a sub-atomic level to a cellular level to a universal level, we are godlike in our ability to create and heal. If I write a book and you see fairies and dragons, and trees that talk in your imagination or out of the corner your eye, I have opened a window to another world for you to consider. I have given energy to an unseen, but nevertheless dynamic secret part of Earth. If this combination is drawn or if it is a part of the comprehensive reading, Spirit wants to applaud your artistic and imaginative endeavors, and ask that you continue creating, and maybe to sing while you do it. They love singing.

Earth/Venus 1 in the 11th House of Universal Loveforce: No means no. This is pretty simple really, but it does take a great deal of courage to say no in the first place and even more when the no is dismissed as *maybe* or *later* or just ignored completely. This is not acceptable. Spirit expects these Earth/Venus 2 people to stand up for themselves and for innocent others. They must become tougher and more assertive (if not downright aggressive) in insisting that they are listened to and that their wishes be respected. Ultimately it may mean that these beings must leave their current situations and start anew with new people who respect each other, honor boundaries, and understand that "no" means "no." Spouses and mates aren't the only abusers of this boundary. Many people seek to intimidate their employees or co-workers if they think they can get away with it. When someone threatens your job or your body, it is time to fight back. Because this aspect is weighed so heavily in the feminine underlying energies of Earth 2, Moon 2, and Venus 2, it might seem fluffy, but it isn't. Those feminine aspects are powerful, proactive, and strong. Sun 2 stands behind this aspect too, so a lot of guidance is provided in how to deal with disrespect. Respect extends to fighting for the planet, and in this position, it is expected that Earth/Venus 2 people advocate for Mother Earth too.

Mars in the 12th House of Karma: Mars Beings have earned their place in the Soulforce Pool if this aspect shows up, and it has taken many battle weary lifetimes to get here. Mars people get to just enjoy life for once with very little or no responsibility to Spirit in their higher lives because they have passed all of the tests with flying colors. The House of Karma always carries a three-fold blessing for great good, and conversely, three-fold problems if pure heart beings are harmed by people of this aspect. The odds of that happening are very low because Mars Beings have learned to love; themselves and others. If they slide into old patterns once in awhile, Spirit will forgive that too, because Mars Beings have "earned increment" from Spirit. Mars Beings are blessed by Spirit, and under Spirit's protection, as are their families.

*Footnote: The book, *Spirit Speaks-the Transformation Connection*, was Spirit's message through Johan Adkins, describing in great detail the mission of the Fleur d'leis.

Neptune in the 1st House of Basis: The House of Basis has, at its center, the energy of the Sun or Godhead, teaching, guiding, and sometimes confusing the Neptunian aspects. What you have operating here are the quintessential polar opposites of the Universe, Lifeforce and Loveforce, working at odds in setting up the groundwork for these individuals. Neptune is always love-based first, and in this House, there is a sharing of heart and mind. Neptune is a contradiction of emotion at best, evidencing deep abiding love but also mistrust: pitting the need for attention and closeness against an equally strong need for distance from loved ones. Add to the mixture Sun's flaky sexual appetites and base behavior, and it might be supposed that a Jekyll and Hyde personality would emerge! Thankfully, this isn't the case. What the Sun's energy does in Neptune is make individuals warmer. Neptune's cold aloofness melts in the Sun. This creates not only people with deep and abiding love but also people who are warm, friendly, and comfortable in their own skin. It is true that Neptunians might have a sardonic sense of humor as a result of the Sun's influence, but it will all be in good, albeit strange, and a little kinky, fun.

Saturn in the 2nd House of Values: This will be a fun household, dramatic and larger than life, with plays in the dining room after supper starring the family dog as the dragon; pure fantasy on parade! Even though these changeable Saturnians may be just one step away from financial disaster, they will keep life interesting for their freedom-loving families, and the ride will definitely be worth it. There is so much love in this household where everyone talks at once but every voice is heard. The décor of the house will likely be flashy, colorful, and stage set eclectic, the kind of place where nobody will bat an eye when dinner guests arrive unexpectedly, dressed up like cowboys. It is very unlikely that this family will raise juvenile delinquents. The children will be extremely well adjusted, albeit a little different than their "normal" friends. But what's normal anyway?

Uranus in the 3rd House of Conscious Mind: Uranus people would do much better if they could learn to get out of their own way. Certain people expect certain behaviors from them, and sometimes it is easier to fall in line with the expectations that others have, and continue to play it out that way, but that isn't how it should be. Uranus Beings could choose to show the other side of themselves: the side that is strong and reliable in a crisis, and the side that can see problems coming, and foresee the solutions to forestall them. Uranus people are powerful, dynamic, and larger than life. They are, in truth, more Elementally balanced than most signs. They just need to play to their strengths, and quit letting the poor expectations of people they may have disappointed in the past keep them from seeking higher ground. Involve yourself with community projects with perfect strangers who haven't judged you for the past or decided for you what "usual and normal" behavior is. These strangers will recognize the strengths you have within. The Transformational Test here is to break the pattern of life lessons getting harder and harder by learning from past mistakes, and accepting responsibility for them. Consider taking on a bigger projects for humanity, and giving without any expectations of getting back, or any thought of being admired for giving. Onward and upward should be the new battle cry!

Minerva in the 4th House of Subconscious Mind: Minerva sits naturally in the 4th House of the Subconscious Mind, but Mars is the underlying energy, and with Mars comes issues of aggression and gross reality. Minerva lives in a rather unreal world of dreams, astral travel,, and sleeping long hours to go to night school, but now those hours have a disquieting aspect. They may see things they don't want to see, and dream things of a prophetic nature that are disturbing. Minervan Beings will be called on by Spirit to intervene in other dimensions and time lines. Their dreams will be realities to whole groups of people, and Minervans may be called upon to protect people from harm. Instead of just nudging those dream people or beings on the right subtle path to good decisions, they may actually have to nudge them to keep them from being harmed or killed. This aspect is a very difficult path for the Minervans because they are warriors at heart too, and have seen their share of gross reality; they just don't like it much, and would rather not deal with it in their dreams. The Spiritual Test here is to not turn away and shut this aspect out. It won't happen all the time, but when it does, it is happening to you because Spirit can count on you to help, so please help.

Sun 2 in the 5th House of Love Aspect: Sun 2 is Creator energy, and understanding the female, and understanding love has always been the bane of his existence. Throughout all of time the Creator, as Zeus, as Wellspring Father, and as any number of hundreds of other names and personas he has worn, has enjoyed the companionship of female mates, but he says he doesn't fully understand females, and probably never will. They are an absolute enigma to him. If you've landed under this aspect, and are male, you definitely experience this same dilemma. If you are a female, you are probably even identifying with this as well. Females in this aspect don't fully understand their sisters either. With Neptune's energy adding an element of playful sexuality and possible kinkiness to this whole equation, it will be a challenge to deal with the basic matter at hand. The Spiritual Test that Wellspring Father keeps having to learn, he says, is to make every effort to get in touch with your feminine side; try to understand the females around you; study them as if they were anthropological test subjects if you have to, and see if you can get a better handle on it than he has. He loves females, and relies on them in every way; he just thinks they are having one over on him half the time.

Moon 2 in the 6th House of Physical Aspect: Our powerhouse Moon 2 aspect just got barraged with extreme ends of planetary influences: Saturn and Venus, Loveforce, and Lifeforce in spades. I say in spades because Saturn's psychic influence upon an already powerful Moon 2 intuitive influence will produce individuals who could top the master sleuths of Miss Marple, Agatha Christie, Sherlock Holmes, or rival the psychic Edgar Cayce. They will be impossible to fool or lie to, and they aren't going to be the type of individuals who lie to themselves. They see themselves as strong, confident, and street smart because of Saturn's influence, and they like the fact that they are unreadable. They show you what they want to, and no more. It gets a little confusing because they will read everyone else, ferreting out every secret, and every confession, and people won't even know what hit them.

Moon 2's here are witty and funny in a quirky way, and nobody quite knows how to take them. It would be wise to take them seriously, because they definitely have others' numbers from the get-go. People will *want* to have the approval of Moon 2 Beings, so they will tell them everything. That's part of the problem. People sense that they can be trusted, and want to get to know them better, and share with them because they sense that Moon 2 beings can help them understand. This is true.

What Moon 2 Beings understand is literally everything. They are psychic enough to be twenty paces ahead of the current situation, and that gets boring. It is the rare individual who does not bore Moon 2 people to distraction, but because Moon 2 Beings are masters at masking their reactions, most people will never know where they truly stand. One thing Spirit needs Moon 2 people to work on is tuning in to the quiet heart: the ones who don't pour out their souls; the ones who are quietly desperate, and need help but won't impose on others to get it. Just because people are silent doesn't mean they aren't in need. Find those people, and be there for them.

Earth/Venus 2 in the 7th House of Emotional Aspects: Wherever Earth and Venus 2 show up, there is a driving need to advocate for the underdog. When these energies show up in the House of Emotions, not only will emotions be heightened and come into play, but they also will come into play amplified by the powerhouse energy of Uranus. Things here could get nasty, but take heart. For Earth/Venus 2 Beings to have made it to this point of spiritual evolution, the Uranus energy sitting behind the 7th House has matured. Also enough so as not to love within, but to be able to extend that love outward in order to put others first. Here's the catch. Nobody better hurt their friends and family or there will be direct consequences. If Earth and Venus 2 are predominant, they will be so proactive in their advocacy for the underdog that they will be entirely consumed with resolving the issue. If Uranus energy predominates, Uranus will not only expose the villains publically, and possibly legally, but this being will be adamant about making said villains pay, hopefully without smashing faces, and property damage. The test here is to allow the love balance that Earth and Venus 2 embrace to soften the hammer blows that Uranus wants to deliver. Earth and Venus 2 will act in the back of these people's minds, handing them a chisel to chip away at the bad guys, and beat them at their game, instead of beating them with a hammer. Uranus can influence others to be proactive as well, and, it is that side that will surface here and triumph in the end.

Mercury in the 8th House of Generation: Mercury Beings are just cute. They are funny, generous, attractive, vital, and a royal pain. They're slippery and hard to hold onto. They like to travel, and they love to interact with everything and everybody, and typically, they don't have to work too hard to have everything come to them. When these people need money for a tip, will simply look down and find $10.00. The Universe answers their needs. Mercury Beings are attractive, so they will attract male or female companions, because, they're just cute. As in Tom Cruise cute. However, this can cause problems, because while they will attract people who burn with desire for them and want to be with them. Mercury Beings are generally clueless about the effect they have on others.

If you've drawn this card, a couple of things could be going on. You may be the Mercury Being to whom all others are attracted; in which case, you need to be aware that you are playing with fire, and must take care not to burn tender hearts who can't resist you. Back off from married people, and behave yourself for the good of the person to whom you are attracted if for no other reason.

If you are the person attracted to Mercury Beings, enjoy the individuals you are attracted to as really good and true friends, however, unless you are both single, don't risk a stable, loving relationships to be together. The Mercury Beings won't stick around, and it is very unlikely they will give up their families for you. Be kind to each other, and don't let it go there.

UNIVERSAL LIFEFORCE CHART 10

10 Sun 1
11 Moon 1
12 Earth/Venus 1
1 Mars
2 Neptune
3 Saturn
4 Uranus
5 Minerva
6 Sun 2
7 Moon 2
8 Earth/Venus 2
9 Mercury

Sun 1 in the 10th House of Universal Lifeforce: This Sun 1 placement is such a balance of heavy-hitting feminine energy that it sets up a perfect yin and yang of the energy of Loveforce/Lifeforce. In the world of Spirit, there are those who are destined to be reincarnated lifetime after lifetime, not because they need to be, but because they want to help do Spirit's work on Earth as an Archangel. If you have this aspect in your Full Chart or Soul Chart, you are one of these beings. You are very aware of who you are. You hear Spirit clearly, and when well balanced, you have probably experienced seeing spiritual entities as well. It is a given that you have "faery sight", and can see subtle changes in wind and sky, and the Earth that tell a story, and expose themselves to you. You've seen the giant faces that direct wind, you've seen the folk in the grasses and trees, and you are blessed to be able to help them if help is asked. This may be a secret part of yourself but what you see that others don't is the interplay of color and light all around, and the sound of the heavens played out in color. It is very likely that you will be called upon to do Spirit's work on Earth, working nightly in Dreamstate to help. This placement is blessed indeed, and the Transformational Test that you will have from Spirit is to play your blessings forward, to be both teacher and student.

Moon 1 in the 11th House of Universal Loveforce: When Moon 1 people grow their souls sufficiently to reach Universal Loveforce, they have already passed many tests of love: giving love, teaching others how to love, and healing with love. Something will happen to light a fire under the need to nurture more than family. At this juncture, they are seeing that love must extend beyond to a much bigger Universal Loveforce picture. The ills of society, our culture, our families, and even many of the ills of our Earth can be healed with love. Moon 1 people have an abundance of knowledge and experience to light the way. They may find that they involve themselves in community service or counseling in some form. They are definitely in a position to mediate problems for other families and communities, to organize awareness programs, or just roll up their sleeves to help build a homeless shelter or man a food bank. They have already done a lot of the hard stuff to earn their transformational place. The energy of the Planet Moon teaches us to understand the natural rhythms of life, to honor the mother, and to honor the teacher within. Moon 1 Beings can expect to be teachers in this life of the aspect of higher love. They are called upon to mother the Earth, mother those who need love, and to promote human existence with love, and for love. Remember, this aspect addresses not what one *intended* to do with their lives but what actually was accomplished. A Spiritual Test would be "When you are sitting at St. Peter's gate, and asking to be let in, what did you do to promote love in the Universe?"

Earth/Venus 1 in the 12th House of Karma: Earth/Venus Beings begin their journey in a house where they can't get away with anything. There is instant karma for any wrongdoing against anything of a pure heart, and to boot, there is a kicker. The harm, negativity, or bad vibes wished upon another return three-fold upon the ill wisher. That's a lot of broken mirrors. The saving grace is that there is also instant three-fold blessings for good work and good thoughts. It is so very unlikely that these people will be anything but loving and giving, and wonderful.

Mars in the 1st House of Basis: These people have been warriors in most of their lifetimes and even in this one, they will experience their fair share of troubles with mates, children, and immediate family. For the most part, Mars Beings aren't fully understood. They do what they need to do to survive, and get along as best they can. These people aren't particularly social, and view other viewpoints, which aren't based in reality, as alien and misguided. They aren't victims, and trying to play that role for very long at all will eventually send them screaming away, about as far away as they can get. It isn't their way to hold their tongue, for very long anyway. Things are better out on the table and talked out, right away. If the ability to work problems out is shoved into the closet or put off for another day, these people will process the situation out of proportion to the problem. If they are forced to hold their tongue to accommodate someone else's needs, they will probably not be able to deal with the situation as rationally as they would have if the problem had just been hashed out when it first arose. On the other hand, they can be good friends to a few people, and that's the way they like it. They must be nurtured in order to love, and they do need to love.

Neptune in the 2nd House of Values: Neptunes in this place won't be easily understood. They will observe the object of their affection for some time before they decide to commit themselves, even in a small way. Neptune Beings will be loving, attentive, and interested in everything, but in the back of their minds, they are like deer in the headlights, looking for reasons to run. They are also looking for reasons to trust that if they are their true selves, they will still be loved.

The same processing takes place with major financial decisions they have to make. When they are young, they may be very rash with cash, and make poor decisions. However, when the Neptunes have reached maturity, and perhaps been "burned" by life a little or a lot, their baby step process kicks in. Any major expenditure of cash will happen only slowly and methodically. It will be researched, and thought out thoroughly before Neptune is comfortable with parting with the cash. These beings aren't stingy, and they aren't afraid to spend where they choose to spend it; they just have to think about it first, and decide what they want the most. Neptune people are firm and strict parents who will tend to show their love by doing things with their children, and taking the time to teach them things.

Saturn in the 3rd House of the Conscious Mind: These people are really hard for others to understand. Their thought processes are very illusive and complex. Saturn people not only think outside the box, but their boxes are multi-dimensional. They are no-nonsense, street smart people, who only look gentle. Both males and females will have the look and behaviors of cats, and will tend to have bodies like gymnasts rather than muscle builders.

Both male and females are deeply aware, and they are watching EVERYTHING and everybody everywhere, trying to get a handle on what *really* is going on. The glib boss or schmoozy car salesmen will never fool them. They have everyone's number, and a firm grasp on the true reality of a situation. Because of this sixth sense, they have to be very careful about what they say: best to lead the clueless from layer to layer until they get a clue too. These Saturnians will make them think it was all their own idea in the first place, and even let them take credit for it!

Uranus in the 4th House of the Subconscious Mind: These beings have sides to their personalities that belong to only them, and In all probability, nobody will ever know them fully. This placement can bring loneliness and isolation. It is the placement of karmic lessons: to tell meticulously the truth or withhold the truth if it causes undue pain, and to refrain from embellishing or dramatizing a situation. Uranus people are always a little leery of strong emotions and anger issues. Keep in mind that if small situations are addressed as they happen, they won't become larger issues that can backfire if handled in an aggressive manner.

It is their test in this lifetime to find balance in the happy medium. These beings learn to ground their excessive energies, learning peace from Mother Earth and love from the aspect of Venus. Learning the aspect of love will allow them to empathize better. One thing that will always help is gardening or doing yard work, and digging in or lying on the Earth to help get things in perspective. Ask for continued guidance from Mother Earth and the love aspect of Venus, and then be receptive to their wise counsel.

Minerva in the 5th House of Personal Love Aspect: People with this placement are looking for more than love; they are looking for a spiritual existence. They may find this love in a larger than life person who is of like mind, but they should wait to commit until they can truly call someone "soul mate." It is very important for these people not to jump into a long-term relationship with someone who can't understand the spiritual aspects of this kind of love. In any event, in order to be at a place where you can recognize your soul mate, some Spiritual, Emotional, and Physical housecleaning must be done with yourself first. Mates have to be capable of much more than being a good friend or just good in bed. They have to touch the soul.

Sun 2 in the 6th House of Physical Aspect: These people never seem to age. They maintain a youthful appearance and mentality their whole lives, and with the masculine energies of Sun 2 and Saturn combined, they exude sexuality, this allows them to attract whatever and whomever they want. There will be enough psychic and intuitive ability from the underlying energy of Saturn to know just what to say, when to say it, and to whom. If Sun Beings believe this to be true, they are deceiving themselves. What may be closer to the truth is that without some constraint, these people can be domineering and pushy. Yes, they are attractive, and yes, they are charming, but neither of the masculine energies involved here is particularly attentive to anyone else's point of view. Other people will be lucky if they have a chance to express a differing opinion without being run over. The best part of this combination is that these Sun Beings are so attractive and charming that most people probably won't mind being trampled. Spirit minds, however, and the lesson here is to practice SILENT observation, and NOT to manipulate people or situations when it is so easy to do so. These Sun folks must learn discernment.

Moon 2 in the 7th House of Emotional Aspect: Women have always known that the cycles of the Moon affect mood and sometimes directly affect their menstrual cycles. The fact that women living together in close proximity will naturally coordinate their menstrual cycles should give us some indication of what is at work here. We are 90% water. We are interconnected water bodies, and the Moon's energy ebbs and flows within us, just as it does the tides. If you have any doubt the power of the Moon, just picture yourself on a tiny boat in the middle of an ocean during a storm. Expect some amplification here in the normal waxing and waning of emotions due to powerhouse energies converging (Sun 2, Moon 2, and Uranus) and try not to let the emotions overwhelm you. Imagine yourself immersed in a nice warm bath, and just enjoy and experience the excess. Don't always try to release emotions: learn to explore them, and allow them to be.

Earth/ Venus 2 in the 8th House of Generation: The Venus lesson for these beings is to love and teach others to love responsibly. They tend to have strong family values, and strong attachments to an extended family. They are tied to Mother Earth and their mothers will be important. They may have a special relationship with Diana or Mother Mary or female Saints or goddess'. It is very likely that males and females will study, and perhaps experiment at some point in their lives with Wicca and magic, or they may have strong ties to Native American spirituality, and walk the Rainbow Way. In some fashion, they will unite with the Earth Mother in whatever spiritual way is meaningful to them.

The Earth/Venus combination makes good, loving parents. Earth element people are usually affectionate, and have healthy sexual interests. They have a great sense of humor, and their laughs and giggles are infectious.

They will always have to watch a tendency to over-eat, and suffer health problems as a result of that, particularly diabetes. They have a tendency when they are disconnected from Earth's energy to depression or ennui. When that happens they need to go outside, and lie in the grass and soak up Sun and Earth energy and more than that. They need to learn to channel Earth energy to others up through the root chakra, which requires them to sit on the Earth, and draw energy up through their bodies.

The Spiritual Test of an Earth/Venus 1 in the House of Generation is to connect deeply with the Earth Mother, promote Loveforce, and stand up for the underdog. The Spiritual Test of an Earth/Venus 2 in the House of Generation is to not only stand up for the underdog, but to advocate, and protect them at possible risk to themselves and everything they love.

Mercury in the 9th House of Regeneration: These Mercurial people dream of travel, and the love of travel will be a lifelong love. These Mercury Beings are the consummate adventurers with the Spirit of James Bond. They may be called upon by Spirit to go on a spiritual journey at some point in their lives. They are blessed of Spirit, and if open, will receive direct spiritual contact and teachings. This contact may require that these people go here, do this, meet this person, and possibly convey a message. Even if they are not open to being directed in their travels, they will nevertheless have the urge to move, and keep moving, constantly. Their favorite vacation would be one in which they could wander around with no set destination, eating when hungry, sleeping when tired, and getting up when they wanted to get up. They can expect at points in their lives to experience the visitation of walking Spirit. Be aware that the person in the right place at the right time lending help or asking for help, might be sent to test you or be there as a messenger or protector.

UNIVERSAL LOVEFORCE CHART 11

11	Sun 1
12	Moon 1
1	Earth/Venus 1
2	Mars
3	Neptune
4	Saturn
5	Uranus
6	Minerva
7	Sun 2
8	Moon 2
9	Earth/Venus 2
10	Mercury

Sun 1 in the 11th House of Universal Loveforce: These peaceful Sun Beings will be given an understanding of the lesson of universal love, joy, and peace. This is a big picture, and a big blessing. It is very possible that the Sun 1 Beings with this placement will spread the message of love and Spirit's teachings to great masses of people if they are so inclined. It is just as likely that they will live their life in quiet anonymity, simply enjoying the blessing of direct spiritual contact and universal teaching. They can keep it to themselves or spread it around. On either path, they will be blessed with direct contact from a higher form or lots of higher forms, depending on their personal belief system. Either way, the blessing extends to giving these people peace. All they have to do is listen and live their lives in such a way as to be able to hear.

Moon 1 in the 12th House of Karma: Mercury is an underlying energy and influence on this placement. Mercury is travel, adventure, and on the negative side, escapism, whether that escape from reality involves drugs, alcohol, or negative adventures on the Earthier side of sexuality. With this placement, there will be immediate karma for things done against the higher good of the individuals or their friends or family. If people with this placement will seek spiritual guidance from the feminine side of themselves or their friends or family, they can follow the natural side of Mercury, just having adventures in whatever they do. Instant karma works both ways here. It can bring great blessings for great good.

Earth/Venus 1 in the 1st House of Basis: Loveforce is the basis for Earth and Venus' energy and the personality in this placement. The key to these people's own well balanced spirituality is to temper love with Lifeforce, the basis for the natural planet of this placement, the Sun. These people will be tested for how deeply they can love unconditionally. The deepest teaching for these people will be to learn that Loveforce alone is not enough because it is ultimately self-serving. Spirit's message is very clear: care enough about yourself and others not to accept harm or abuse. Run if you can, but be ready to fight back if you have to and protect those who cannot or will not protect themselves.

On a more positive note, these people will act as peacemakers and hold their families together with gluey love. They are best suited to teaching a loving aspect to others. They will be the one relied upon in a crisis to always be the loving hands and the caring individuals. Their love is deep and abiding.

Start here

Mars in the 2nd House of Values: Mars Beings are the ones whom everyone will remember loving and hating. They will always have to watch that warlike tendencies don't wound inappropriately, and will need to curb the need to lash out, saying what might be hurtful. Love will always be battling with family discord here. There are likely to be problems relating to women and mother figures in this aspect. Mars can exert an intimidating influence on others. When this energy is placed in the House of Values, these people will find it too easy to slide over acceptable levels of social behavior, morality, and the grey areas of finance.

The saving grace is that Moon's underlying influence puts love first. If tough love is needed, the strength to give it is here. Teachers born here are a tough nut, but they are the ones who will be able to handle the rougher students and problems that send others away screaming.

Neptune in the 3rd House of Conscious Mind: Neptune's energy is that of the highest form of love, protection, and self-sacrifice. In the House of the Conscious Mind, love will be foremost. Everything is perceived from the viewpoint of a loving outlook, so the natural home of Venus and Earth fall in naturally with this placement. Neptunians in this aspect may have difficulty distinguishing reality from fantasy. They may have visions, psychic inclinations, or dreams that are prophetic in nature. Many times they deal with the love aspect being abused or in need of healing. The one aspect that will have to be ultimately accepted by these Neptune Beings is that the underdog will often require their protection. There will be necessary battles to fight. No fence sitting is allowed if someone else may be hurt by inaction.

Neptunes in this placement must also watch out for self-pitying or destructive behaviors, which may come when they try to mentally process too much. If individuals with this placement get overwhelmed or seem to be heading down this path, the prescription is a day in nature, in the Sun. They need to get back to the Earth, balance and regroup, and ask Spirit or God to quiet the mind for a time and provide some perspective.

Because of the ultimate femininity of this sign, a male with this aspect should be able to communicate beautifully with females and will be accepted widely in feminine circles. However, relating to the male machismo personality of others may be difficult for him. A female with this placement will have a trusted group of female friends, but many women will mistrust Neptune's ultimate female vibes. When these people look at the physical and emotional side of life from afar, they may see this loving tendency as a weakness, but it is not. Loveforce is strong and can melt the hardest heart if the heart is capable of understanding true love.

Saturn in the 4th House of the Subconscious Mind: These people will be always be battling their emotional and psychological demons and must constantly guard against negativity ruling their lives. They must teach themselves not to react until they can process.

This complex person understands subtle layers and connections and can see through deception and lies. They understand the criminal mind. Just because the Saturn Being can see levels and layers of gross imbalance, this skill doesn't necessarily make them the bad guy, although the potential is there if they don't stay balanced. They are singularly placed to expose and do battle with darker energies because they have to constantly fight to defeat the darkness in themselves.

Some people, sensing darkness within, become afraid of themselves and may immerse in extreme or cultish behavior to try to drown out or purge these underlying dark thoughts. That mind set is self-deception and illusion. The ability to understand dark thoughts and actions is a gift that can be turned to good. They might be the perfect person to understand, find or fight the bad guys, or heal the bad guys because nobody will spot darkness as well as they do in this placement The ability to recognize and fight gross imbalance or turn it around and heal it is their Spiritual Test. The ability to actually fight the darkness and corruption and destroy it is a Fleur d'leis cleansing process. See the book, *Spirit Speaks-the Transformation Connection* for Fleur d'leis training.

Uranus in the 5th House of Love Aspect: Love is never easy. It is especially hard for people who see themselves as loving and giving but seem to be susceptible to others' using that love to manipulate and hurt. Love then becomes something else. It becomes not-love. Unfortunately, there are many people out there who have been hurt and think that pretending or feigning love as a means to get what they want, or to get back at someone else who hurt them. The lesson for this placement: dump anyone who would abuse love this way. Don't waste love on those who are unable to love. Don't waste love on someone who would use and abuse you in the name of love. Spirit's test for you here is to love yourself enough to reject unloving ways. Don't give too much of yourself until the measure of an individual and the love they offer is proved genuine. If you are already in a situation, make the decision to stay or go a totally selfish one. Don't consider the abuser's needs; just seek your own peace and happiness.

Minerva in the 6th House of Physical Aspect: Transformational states in the House of Physical Aspect and self-perception is seemingly another contradictory concept, but it is not. We are moving out of our physical bodies, not only at the end of our physical lives, but at this time of spiritual trial and judgment. We are preparing for oneness with Spirit and winding up our Earthly incarnations to learn the final lessons we have set for ourselves lifetime after lifetime. Throw off the old judgments of others and embrace the acceptance of alternative paths.

Earth is the place of physical, emotional and spiritual trial and in this aspect you have reached the Earthly incarnation that will test your spiritual mettle. To move forward to Nirvana states or wisdom states, this life "upheaval" is a necessary process. The test of success and Earthly successful transformational state is the opening of the Hocaieah, the twin healing chakras located just under the collarbone. This is the time of life that we need to do a spiritual, emotional, and physical "housecleaning." Throw off the judgments of others and embrace the acceptance of alternative paths. Accept a new look, new ideas, and new philosophies. Sift through all the baggage and literally jettison what doesn't fit. Simplify, unify, purify, and balance. Dance, sing, and be happy. This process isn't comfortable. It often involves dredging up your personal "demons" and finally deal with them. People in transformational states must forego the judgment of others. Part of foregoing judgment is not accepting blame for the circumstances in the Life Path of other adults. Minerva Beings must learn to release control to be free.

Sun 2 in the 7th House of Emotional Aspects: People who have drawn this combination are struggling to understand the emotional picture of their day-to-day situations and their relationships in general. It is as if everyone else is an alien and has a view askew from the reality that people with this aspect share. It is probable that misunderstandings will ensue due to a lack of empathy to emotional turmoil, but these are the same people who can provide a cool head and straight thinking in a crisis, so hopefully the family and friends will be forgiving.

Moon 2 in the 8th House of Generation: After this many incarnations in their Earthly physical life, these Moon 2 beings are becoming warmer individuals, more in tune with the emotions and needs of others and caring a bit more about socially appropriate dress. The biggest change in their higher-self work is their ability to more fully explore the richness of their dream lives. They've learned to slip in and out of other dimensions either in sleep phase or astral projection. They've also honed their skills of empathy and sympathy and are learning to not only "walk" in the shoes of another, but to psychically sense in projection where pain and suffering enter and what to do to help. This is a very exciting and vital association because Minerva can transmute whatever energy these individuals need when they need it, exponentially increasing the ability for the Earthly individual to help heal anything. Spirits' test for this placement is to put those skills to work to help others heal themselves and help Spirit heal everything. Be on the lookout for entities who are in trouble.

Earth/Venus 2 in the 9th House of Regeneration: The House of Regeneration is a house of ascension, but in order for Earth/Venus 1 individuals to get there, they have to learn a great deal in this lifetime and be on this path for awhile. They have to be balanced Elementally and male to female; they have to have experienced the rise of kundalini; and they have to pass the tests of the Fleur d'leis.*(See footnote). People earning this status can join the Soulforce Pool after this incarnation. Needless to say, the tests are tough, but the attempt is well worth the journey. It is transcendence. If you are this Earth/Venus person, be prepared to work hard and know that you are blessed to be doing this work.

Mercury in the 10th House of Universal Lifeforce: Mercury was a messenger of the Gods depicted as having wings on his feet. In their most secret hearts, people with this placement want wings too. They want to take a message and travel with it to the ends of the Earth. Winged feet confined by shoes often long to run barefoot and take flight on their own. If they have something they want to say, then it must be said at some point in their lives, even if it has to be secretly. If these people do not literally travel to spread the message, they must branch out to friends and family and perhaps wider groups of people to share the message where they can.

Maybe these people will write or promote a book, or maybe they will believe so strongly in a political, religious, or social ideal that they will devote their lives to promoting it. THAT means that these people have the ability to influence others. They can sell what they promote and believe in. It is a natural gift.

*Fleur d'leis explanation: "Flower of Lifeforce" in the stone or Pen'l Leina-Language, an older spelling than fleur de lys. What this spiritual training involves is taking a deep look at, and cleansing of any residual hatreds or a sense of things left undone, in order to forgive, forget, or let go and move on. These beings will have Physical, Emotional, and Spiritual Tests to pass. The book, Spirit Speaks-the Transformation Connection, channeled in part to

Johan Adkins, gives very specific instructions on how to find out where you are on this journey. The Fleur d'leis teaching is also available there. When people achieve this status, they will feel an increased awareness; they can move energy in any direction; they have the ability to hear and see Spirit; and they have increased ability to work with the Elements, Vortex, and the creatures of Earth, sea, and sky. They are able to deal with negative energy and transmute or destroy it if necessary. Their skill at creative visualization is extremely powerful, and their higher selves can literally create what they imagine for the Universe; this requires mature and forward-thinking analysis of the situation. Their abilities to heal all things will increase, and they will have an innate understanding of what to do. They will really earn their spiritual symbol of the fleur de lys. This traditional French symbol represents many things, but historically it is a symbol of protection and honor.

KARMA CHART 12

12	Sun 1
1	Moon 1
2	Earth/Venus 1
3	Mars
4	Neptune
5	Saturn
6	Uranus
7	Minerva
8	Sun 2
9	Moon 2
10	Earth/Venus 2
11	Mercury

Sun 1 in the 12th House of Karma: All souls returning to a new incarnation start here. Although it is the Twelfth House, it is actually the first house that individuals come to after deciding what they will be learning, teaching, and experiencing between one lifetime and another. This Being may have already evolved into the Soulforce Pool and is returning as an Angel on Earth for a specific task; or It may still be working on balancing itself elementally or in its incarnations as male and female. Incarnations still earning Soulforce Pool transformation must ultimately balance these male and female incarnations in order to fully incorporate the masculine and feminine energies in their being. For a soul who has just spent many lives as male and is now a female, it can be difficult to reconcile the feminine within themselves or understand the feminine in others. Incarnating as a male after many feminine lives can also be confusing, but people in this aspect are perhaps more balanced male to female because they have recent spiritual memory of what the feminine means.

On top of this, there is the matter of dealing with a new Elemental teacher. All souls have a primary Lifescript Elemental guide, but if they are having difficulty, it may be because the souls aren't used to their Elemental in this incarnation. If there are a lot of anger issues, for example, it may be because a Water Being isn't used to the force of the Fire Element in this incarnation on top of its primary Elemental guide. We must ultimately deal with all six Elements in their time in the span of our lives. This is what it means to be balanced Elementally: we live with and learn from all six Elements. One clue as to what Element is currently prominent is one's "favorite" color. Look in your closet and see if there isn't a color clue!

Moon 1 in the 1st House of Basis: The energy of the Moon as Loveforce and the underlying energy of the Sun as Lifeforce is in perfect balance in this placement. These people will have the energy to create and will feel inspired to do so. They have the perfect opportunity with this solid base to accomplish anything they desire as long as they stay balanced. They can expect to have guidance to do what is right. If they are imbalanced male to female and/or elementally, they must guard against the ability to "hear" guidance to do what is wrong. With this placement of power, negative influences are drawn to try to influence and confuse the issues. It would be advisable for the Moon people to be aware and surround themselves with love and light, using the threefold protection mantra, "I will hear only that which is of pure heart and love and light. I close my perception and my hearing to that which is not pure of heart." Mantras of communication with Spirit need to be repeated three times: once to state the intention, once to get the attention of Spirit, and once to seal the intention.

Earth/Venus 1 in the 2nd House of Value: Earth/Venus Beings love homes that reflect their personality. They love to dress up; they love to give; and they especially love to shop for EVERYTHING. The Spiritual Test for Earth/Venus 1 people in the House of Values will be tough. At some point in their lives, they will need to figure out why they give and how they can shift their values away from possessions.
The Spiritual Test for the Earth/Venus 1 in the House of Values, will be to restructure your life to live within your means, budget, and plan for emergencies. Rough test. With this placement, it is not traditional to have sufficient savings to take care of unforeseen expenses…and you do love beautiful things.

When the symbiotic energy of the kundalini rises, generally during the forties or fifties, a shift in spiritual perception will ensue. This shift prompts these individuals to do a physical, emotional, and spiritual housecleaning as well as an actual physical house cleaning. They will need to part with things in order to move out from under a suffocating feeling. When the excess is cleared and cleaned away, the suffocating feelings will be too.

Mars in the 3rd House of Conscious Mind: Mars, male or female, always has difficulty understanding the feminine, except in this aspect. Earth and Venus are ganging up and lending lots of grounding and Loveforce to balance these individuals more fully, male to female and Lifeforce to Loveforce. This can produce warrior spirits with a more humane aspect who will not allow people to be harmed arbitrarily or allow a family to be separated. They will be a natural negotiator and will try to solve problems with discussion and mediation rather than allow needless harm, chaos, or discord. They have a gift for smoothing ruffled feathers because they are empathetic and can walk a mile in anyone's shoes. Mars Beings can be strong and forceful, never doubt it; and they may hide their more caring side, but it is there. It would be well for the people to remember to step lightly around their feelings. They can definitely be hurt by a cavalier attitude implying that they are uncaring towards the family or expressing a feminine point of view on emotional issues. Unfortunately, even here, mixed signals may be given because Mars Beings may not have the courage to be themselves and allow some of their sappier thoughts and spontaneous actions to surface.

If you have drawn this card two things can be going on: either you are trying to understand a strong individual who is giving mixed signals or you are this individual and are giving mixed signals. In any event, you aren't showing your true self and it may be time to allow some of the sappier thoughts and spontaneous actions to surface. If you are looking at this to help understand why your Mars friend is acting strangely and is dressing up for Halloween and going to musicals, you'd better be supportive! Male or female, we cannot be whole without embracing both feminine and masculine energies.

A Spiritual Test in this aspect is to be who and what you are without hiding anything you think people will reject. Balancing the male and female can be subtle and it can be done in the privacy of your home. If you are in public, be yourself, and don't be afraid that your fellows will mock you. You are a born negotiator and mediator, and really, your friends don't care. They are secretly wishing they understood people as well as you do.

Neptune in the 4th House of Subconscious: This placement is quite unique and wonderful for Neptune Beings. Neptune's natural energy signature is usually overwhelmed and inherently imbalanced by Loveforce energy alone, but when it combines with the inherently imbalanced Lifeforce energy of Mars, the underlying energy of the 4th House, both Neptune aspects and Mars aspects balance each other out perfectly. Neptune Beings get to find peace and acceptance and they are open enough to learn from night school lessons. This injects a new vitality and energy into the equation that generates more confidence. What is unseen is a natural tendency to aspire to greatness that is always held back by basic insecurity; but not here. This is a big deal because it means that the insecurities of Neptune and the aggression of Mars synergize into something else altogether:

passion, vigor, energy, and a drive to accomplish. These people will be so charismatic they can accomplish just about anything they set their mind to. They make excellent lawyers, advocates, teachers, and actors, and they will have a will to excel. There is just enough of the Neptune need for attention and acceptance that they will probably eventually end up in the public eye, in politics, or in some arena of the entertainment field. If they take on a project, it will be done and done well. Spirit's test in this endeavor is to teach Neptunians what it feels like to be balanced so that in future transformational movements, they can draw on their experience of one perfect lifetime in which they were "shiny."

Saturn in the 5th House of Love Aspect: Saturn People seem like the perfect mates, charming and life loving as they can be, but there is always another side to the love equation with them: they are extremely intuitive, if not downright psychic, so there will be no opportunity for potential mates to deceive them. On the other hand, they themselves can be the masters of deception, the caped crusaders attracting potential lovers or mates like flies. Saturnians are looking for someone who can touch their souls. Saturn people live their lives a slight step off the planet. By that token, they may seem a little spacey and distracted, when in all probability they are sifting through a lot of potential realities to check where they are landing. If their reality for love includes you, you are lucky indeed. Peter Pan has landed on you!

Uranus in the 6th House of Physical Aspect: Uranus gets a break here. Saturn is the underlying energy, and it adds playful, fun, and intuitive life to what is usually a very heavy normal existence for Uranus. Uranus Beings finally have great possibility for healthy and happy relationships and their marriages will run much smoother. However, because Uranus people are so strong, they will need to find very understanding mates who can handle an individualistic go-getter. These folks are always juggling many projects at a time and they approach life with an enthusiasm for excellence. This is great, except for the fact that they tend to burn themselves out and will require periods of down time. It takes awhile in each lifetime for Uranus to make themselves stop and smell the roses without feeling the need to re-design the flowerbed into three acres of a labyrinth. Once they figure out how to make themselves relax and step away from obsessively working 24/7, they'll be much happier. The Spiritual Test is to stop and smell those roses and pick them for someone who needs a "pick me up." Get out of yourself occasionally and support the ones around you who have supported you so often. Take them some roses!

Minerva in the 7th House of Emotional Aspect: Minerva is the Dreamweaver, and she sits here in a house that is ruled by Uranus. Emotions run strong in mutable directions; therefore, an Element Card should be pulled here to understand the direction this aspect will take you at this time. This is the only aspect that requires readers to fill in some of their own gaps with an outside source. Minerva's energy is unlike any in the Universe. It is mutable, meaning that it molds itself against the need of a flowing river to help adjust the ebb and flow of the balance of Lifeforce and Loveforce, so it is always changing just as emotions change.

If you have drawn this card in response to a question and intend to just read one aspect, then here is the situation: emotions are out of control and you need to take some time to determine how to rein them in. If you aren't getting any rest and you are processing too much, Spirit suggests that you ground and center and choose an Element Card to help you determine which element you lack that will help settle you or the situation down.

If you have drawn this card in a full reading or comprehensive reading, then here is the situation: there is a teacher available to help you with the emotions surrounding your situation right now and that teacher is the Element Card you will draw right now. It is possible that you have too much of the Element you will draw and it is possible you have too little, but the guidance you need to handle what you are dealing with is within the Element you pull.

Sun 2 in the 8th House of Generation: The Sun Beings in the 8th House of Generation are struggling with issues of faith. They are struggling with the day to day, and feeling out of step with it. They are also struggling with having to be the responsible people upon whom everyone depends because it is oppressive. Minerva influences this placement and Minerva has itchy feet. At the same time that Sun people try to be good employers, employees, husbands, wives, or parents, they are wanting and needing to run away from it all, and may sabotage their own success or advancement in a job if it is too demanding or oppressive. They are not necessarily irresponsible or uncaring, but they can be.

On a deep inherent level they feel that they must have a great deal of alone time in order to regroup and recoup their busy minds. Someone trying to look over their shoulder or micromanage any of their efforts will make Sun Beings extremely unhappy and ineffective. Unreasonable deadlines and honey-do lists will drive them to distraction.

Sometimes the families will just have to understand that these individuals have to get completely away from the everyday, everything and everybody for a few days. The Sun Beings may have a completely different set of friends with whom they enjoy a certain amount of freedom. The families should allow the Sun Beings their secret pals or societies. They will come back ready to face their responsibilities again but must be allowed some freedom and breathing room.

These individuals are often spacey and distracted and have a tendency to day dream. They have a lot of unanswered questions that only they can answer. In this lifetime they are tasked with cleaning their spiritual, emotional, and physical houses, and this requires parting with negative, clinging friends and relatives, and eliminating as many material goods (except toys) as possible.

Moon 2 in the 9th House of Regeneration: Diana, the Creator's mate, was given responsibility for the Moon and the Earth. She sees the souls first after death, and is responsible for helping them in rather a limbo stage between lives to determine where they will go next. If they have cleaned up their spiritual houses, they may be ready to join the Soulforce Pool, but if there are lessons they want to learn or if they desire another physical life, they must incarnate. Before they do, they task themselves with the lessons they must learn and others agree to help them by assuming roles in their lives as mothers, fathers, husbands, etc. In this House of Regeneration, and at this stage of transformational maturity, these people may be tasked by Spirit to return as Angels with a specific job to do. These people have the Creator's attention, and if they are very well balanced, they can talk to him. What they need to ask, however, might surprise them. They need to ask the Creator, "What can I do for you?"

Earth/Venus 2 in the 10th House of Universal Lifeforce: Spirit has gifted this wisdom, and it is not what is accepted mythology and Christian understanding. According to Spirit in a channeling, Aphrodite was the daughter of Zeus and Diana, and she and Adonis came to Earth to begin life here. The original Adam and Eve. Adonis was fully formed when he came to exist. Janus is always depicted as two males, but the true face of Janus can't be seen by mere mortals or Angels or Archangels even, for it is the face of the Creator who, at one time called himself Zeus. Zeus split his energy to give the world the best parts of himself. He created what we could term now, a programmed clone, and called him Adonis. Adonis has had many names, but most of us know him as God. Like Janus, it is no surprise that we also have two faces. We are all both male and female and in this House of Universal Lifeforce, we are being called to keep the balance equal between the two parts of ourselves. Those who dwell in this position are tasked with harder lessons of protecting and being proactive for the innocent. They must advocate for the underdog. They must love the unloved and defend the weak. Whether they are male or female, they evolve to become the ultimate mother and father.

Mercury in the 11th House of Universal Loveforce: Wellspring Father was weary of the responsibility of his creations but had to make sure they were cared for. Adonis had the responsibility of their care. Mercury is just one persona of a God created by the Sun, Wellspring Father. Adonis was Mercury's other name, and he had to be responsible for the Universe. That's a big job, especially when he had to balance, universally, the two energies of Loveforce and Lifeforce. To facilitate that, Adonis was given free rein to do what he needed to do. Over the centuries, it was apparent that Loveforce alone corrupted itself, it became either too selfish to sacrifice oneself for another and share their energies, or too literal in the "Thou shall not kill" area. If an innocent is being harmed it is intrinsically necessary to protect the innocent, by fighting, if necessary, or killing if necessary. Certainly, one cannot stand by and do nothing when an innocent is being harmed, and that is what essentially happened in the Universe with pure Loveforce...with one exception, Venus Beings understood what that love meant by protecting others even with their lives.

So the solution was to merge the energies to balance Loveforce with Lifeforce and a universal dance ensued to mingle the energies. It really wasn't easy to do as the Planets were, at one time, divided Loveforce and Lifeforce. So all of life had to change and that change came about in 1994 with the Jupiter comet. Because, if the planets did not accept the basic energy change, life in the Universe would have ended instead of the comet breaking up on Jupiter. If it had hit in one place, it would have knocked Jupiter out of its orbit and it would have knocked the other planets in our solar system out of kilter and that would have been the end of life on planet Earth. Luckily, they all got into line by accepting a change in their energies, except Jupiter.

For the people drawing this card, all of this explanation is necessary, because you are facing a Universal test of Loveforce. An event, or series of events will happen that will make it necessary to stand up for something important, or someone else. You may not actually have to fight or kill, but you must not turn a deaf ear or a blind eye to either violence or mistreatment of a fellow being. It won't necessarily be another human being, it may be a mistreated animal. The other Spiritual Test here is to become more aware of the needs around you. Watch the struggle around you and help.

QUICK PLANETARY GUIDE

Sun 1

Sun 1 General Reading

Sun energy gives spiritual direction straight from the Creator. These people are beloved of Spirit and are blessed throughout their lifetime with the possibility of direct communication with the Creator if they are well balanced. Additionally, they may speak to any and all life forms across all dimensions. These people have the potential to use these gifts to talk to the animals, planets, Angels or anyone else they want to. If they remain open and receptive they will hear direct dialogue from above. They are tasked in this lifetime to stay receptive to need and can utilize vast amounts of energy to direct healing or help where and when needed. Creative visualization and light work is key: what can be imagined can be manifested. They have the potential to heal a cell or a Universe and as such they are destined to try to fulfill Spirit's directives. The harder they try, successful or not, the greater the happiness afforded to them in this blessed existence. It may not be easy, but oh, the things they can learn!

Key Words: Godhead; Spiritual Pool; I am; The Light; Protection.

Key Phrases: Direct spiritual influence; Lifeforce teaching; the basis for all spiritual teaching coming directly from the Creator; ability to see truth through anything.

Energy Signature: Sun is Lifeforce and all the other Planets lend the balance of Loveforce.

Challenges to face: Learn not to always take the easy road. Do the hard things.

Transformational Test: Face the Sun 2 Transformational Test as indicated by the Houses. Spirit will communicate with individuals in Sun 1 and Sun 2 placements, so this test is to become sufficiently balanced and aware in order to hear. It may also be a test of opening up to avenues and tools available to help.

MOON 1

Moon 1 General Reading

The Moon has always been for lovers, and lovers make up Moon placements too. The Moon Beings love almost everything and everybody. They love their family around them and they love beautiful things in their warm homes. They love to spend and probably love to gamble, but they probably don't like dealing with disastrous finances as a result. In order to grow and transcend, the Moon people have to be able to say no to themselves and others and they must resist making cookies for troubled teens and get tough if need be. Tough love is extremely hard for Moon people, because whether they are male or female, they are tied to the feminine aspects of nurturing and mothering. They tend to be the peacekeepers, and they have a calming effect on every situation. However, it can't all be "give, give, give," without getting something back. It is a strange dynamic, that people so gifted with mothering others may subjugate their own needs and sometimes their own personality in order to meet the perceived needs of others. A very hard Transformational Test is to successfully resist doing that. Moon Beings must respect themselves and command respect from willful children who play upon their soft hearts. Moon people must learn to be assertive, and when dealing with others, must learn to be tougher cookies.

Key Words: Changeable; Mother; mother influence; teacher; natural rhythms; natural inclinations. Huntress Diana, Diana of Ephesus

Key Phrases: Attitude towards the Earth and motherhood in general; way of raising children; way of looking at nurturing; way of healing, Diana of Ephesus multiple breasted mother of us all.

Energy Signature: Loveforce/Lifeforce

Challenges: Spending habits, financial challenges

Transformational Test: These people must learn to live within their budget and let go of the material pleasures and some of the comforts in order to transform. They must be balanced Elementally and male to female. They must serve others and put others first. Love has to be tempered with strength of a different kind, and that is parental consistency and tough love when necessary, and standing strong in the possibility of rejection. That is a very hard test for loving Moon people.

EARTH /VENUS 1

Earth General Reading

Mother Earth is alive, but not doing very well. We are polluting her skies and her water and disturbing magnetic forces of the ley-lines by irresponsible fracking and over-mining of minerals. Minerals and metals are placed where they are supposed to be in order to keep the energy of the Earth flowing. They also help the Earth receive energy from the Sun and other Planets as well as give energy reciprocally to keep our solar system in orbit. Yes, we have a big problem and although the world didn't end in December 2012, we may have only bought ourselves a short period of time before the Earth can no longer sustain life. The seas are being polluted and the marine animals who lend their energy to healing the oceans are being overfished and poisoned. Nobody wants to hear this, but it is the critically important job of Earth people to advocate for Mother Earth and to stand up for her. Earth/Venus people need to be actively working on healing the Earth and the seas and work to undo blockages in the Earth's ley-lines, sending healing where it is needed. A mother must protect her young. In order to help Mother Earth protect *our* young, Earth/Venus1 people must first protect her.

EARTH

Key Words: Grounding; home values; balance; individuality

Key Phrases: Way of looking at Earth's needs and meeting Earth's needs; Way of seeing self integral to family; Way of mothering; Attitude toward Earth changes and weather changes; Attention to detail; Advocate of the innocents.

Energy Signature: Lifeforce/Loveforce and Loveforce/Lifeforce.

Challenges: Self-destruction; depression; almost comatose behavior when overwhelmed.

Transformational Test: Earth/Venus people must advocate for others who are being abused, even when the victims won't advocate for themselves. Earth/Venus Beings must place the well-being of innocents above that of the accepted status quo, even at the risk of making themselves unpopular and uncomfortable in their jobs or even within their own families. These people must become so aware of Earth's planetary health that they can feel energy moving through Earth's poles. Corruption will feel like a breakdown along ley-lines of the Earth to Earth/Venus people. They must work with Spirit to actively heal the Earth and possibly other planets in our solar system. They must be balanced Elementally as well as male to female.

Mars

Mars General Reading

Mars Beings are basically lonely warriors. They are trained to fight and to react with swift aggression but when the fighting is over, they are expected to return to society and leave that training behind. The disconnection these people go through when they come home from battle seems to set them up for difficulties in social situations and with their families. Depending on the experiences they may have had in the military, they often suffer from PTSD or have horrible nightmares. While not all Mars Beings have military experience, a strong Mars is still someone weighted heavily in the area of the head and not the heart. As our higher selves, we may have been warriors in other dimensions and certainly have been warriors in previous lifetimes, so we can identify with their struggle. Spirit's test for the tenacious Mars Beings is to channel aggression into fighting battles on the home front that need to be fought while still working on being loving. To champion an innocent is the greatest victory of all.

Key Words: Aggression; war-like; warrior; tenacious

Key Phrases: Warlike tendencies; discord; family dysfunction; social dysfunction; tendency to process and get upset.

Energy Signature: Lifeforce/Lifeforce Lifeforce/Loveforce

Challenges: Mars must learn to separate the work they do from the love aspect and love through all the pain without losing the ability to love.

Transformational Test: This is the area of discord and the House signs showing this discord or imbalance are the areas that have to be worked on for self and family happiness. Mars Beings have to learn to let go of hatreds and embrace self-sacrifice for the sake of others. They must learn the Lessons of Love and use their Warrior nature to right abuse and conquer darkness at extreme levels. Their true test is to do all of this and still love.

Neptune

Neptune General Reading

Dolphins and whales sing healing to the Universe. From under the seas they sit in two dimensions and work tirelessly to heal Loveforce energy for planet Earth, for the spiritual realms, and for every transcended being on the planet. Neptune Beings will forever be tied to water bodies and the Water Element, for they sense their responsibility to work with Loveforce energy to keep things flowing. Their feelings ebb and flow too; they push away, and then pull toward. They are powerhouses in Loveforce energy and when their minds are made up, they are a force to be dealt with. Neptune Beings will always feel a need to test relationships to see if they can be broken. It isn't cruelty; it's self-preservation. Neptunes probably won't be able to keep themselves from playing games with their loved ones and associates in an effort to test the strength and durability of the commitment others have to them. They are also overbalanced towards Loveforce energy that drives an insistent need for attention and proof of love in every relationship they have. Merfolk were always depicted as beautiful men and women whose siren song lured sailors into the sea where they would drown them; and there is a reason behind that myth. Neptune aspects represent sexuality, promiscuity, self-destructive behavior, and destructive behavior generally when they show up in most Houses. Neptune beings must lose their ego and reach selflessness by the 11th House of Loveforce to reach transcendence.

Key Words: Insecurity; self-love; individualist; rebel; high-maintenance.

Key Phrases: Remote viewing. Tests loved ones to see if they will stay.

Energy Signature: Loveforce/Loveforce Loveforce/Lifeforce.

Challenges: Problems with self-esteem; mistrust of others; the contrivance of personal barriers to keep people from getting too close; possible sexual promiscuity. This is the part of all of us that wants to run away when we feel like we don't fit in, feel unwelcome, or feel uncomfortable; the jumping off place for actions that will keep us from fitting in; what people will do to assert their individuality.

Transformational Test: These people must sacrifice physical and individual desires to put their energy into someone or something else of a higher nature; this may call for celibacy or long periods of being alone. These people must learn the true lesson of love and trust.

Saturn

Saturn General Reading

Saturn Beings aren't like other people. They are so sensitive and psychic that they sometimes can't tell what is real from what is fantasy, or what most people think is fantasy. They are dimensional thinkers. Their reality is not what others perceive. Saturn Beings must try to sift through psychic perceptions and messages to ascertain pertinent data and then communicate in a normal conversational way. If they fail at this, they will be misunderstood and possibly thought of as insane or far too eccentric. Saturns' thought processes are complex. They see layers and layers of possible understanding and misunderstanding and they amplify the potential for confusion by talking...and talking...and talking. They can easily dominate the conversation in a whole room, even when nobody else has a clue what the Saturn Being is going on about. Saturn has to stay grounded or else he or she can be perceived as incoherent or even rude. Don't get me wrong; most people love to hear them go on. They are complex and fascinating people. They definitely think outside the box and they are often theatrical and dramatic, not only in their conversational style but also in their dress. They have a youthful appearance and a fun, vibrant attitude that is catching. They would make great super-spies, writers, or actors and they can definitely be the life of a party! The Spiritual Test for these beings is to quiet themselves, center and ground, and take time to sift through the psychic babble to uncover Spirit's messages to them. They will be expected to act on these messages, whether there is something they can do psychically to pass along Spirit's message, or something they can do physically to accomplish a task, like making a Superman cape so that they can visit a daycare and make one little child smile. You never know.

Key Words: Probably psychic; possibly eccentric; chameleon-like; changeable; forever young; individualistic wardrobe; complex; talker; raconteur

Key Phrases: These people experiences layers of understanding, subtle and elusive to others. They crave mystery and intrigue, hence superspy-like fascination. Super-ego; thinking outside the box; strong spiritual perceptions. These people retain a youthful appearance and attitude throughout life.

Energy Signature: 4 times Lifeforce/Loveforce, Loveforce/Lifeforce

Challenges: These people has to avoid the tendency to babble and dominate conversation. They may be or tend to become self-absorbed and self-deluded. Their complex, hard to understand layers of thought and perception confuse even day–to-day issues. The Saturn Being must try to sift through psychic perceptions and messages to ascertain pertinent data and then communicate in a normal conversational way.

Transformational Test: This is the area of psychic perception and how it is used. The test is to develop and then compartmentalize the psychic gifts in order to learn to live a more normal life. These people have the potential to be a great actor or writer, and Spirit may call upon them to use these gifts.

URANUS

Uranus General Reading

Spirit has a lot of hope for Uranus Beings. They have really been "through it." Uranus has twenty times the Lifeforce/Loveforce energy, and these beings traditionally set very hard tasks for themselves in their Life Path plans. The Planet Uranus has taken on the reputation of being the Planet that provides obstacles. Uranus Beings, like determined and faithful drill sergeants, choose to put themselves and others through the paces. The reward for success, however, is great.

There is a hierarchy in Spirit, and one of the most sought after placements in the Soulforce Pool is that of the Creator's trusted inner guard: the Walkers. Uranus Beings aspire to earn status here because it means that they will literally be powerful enough to shift energy from planet to planet or mend the matrix of the Universe with a thought. They seek to do something else as well: help other war weary and tortured souls find peace. The way they do this is by understanding, more than any other being, what it means to fight alone against incredible odds. These are the Spirit Guides of soldiers and protectors. Once Uranus Beings transcend from this point, Spirit has special tasks for them as they finally earn their place in the Soulforce Pool: either returning as Angels on Earth to help others in their transformational paths or joining the Soulforce Pool to actively work to balance the Universes. Uranus will be Metal affiliated, and that's a big deal. They will be able to join the Creator in journeys to repair the matrix that holds the Universe together.

Key Words: Heavy energy, warrior, moody

Key Phrases: Yo-yo emotions and behavior; seems to make the same mistakes.

Energy Signature: 20 x Lifeforce/Lifeforce, Lifeforce/Loveforce, Loveforce/Loveforce

Challenges: Burdens; obstacles; increasingly difficult obstacles for self and others if karmic lessons aren't learned; caring too much what others think; exhibits yo-yo emotions sometimes resulting in inappropriate reaction or behavior.

Transformational Test: The Uranus Beings will keep having the same things happen until they learn to get out of their own way and stop blaming others as the cause of their problems. Lifeforce and Loveforce lessons of this life not learned get extremely harder in subsequent lifetimes and more demanding of attention. Maybe Uranus Beings must finally hit bottom unless they get a clue to trust in their higher-self, to "Let go, and let God." This is an extremely difficult lesson for them. The rewards for learned lessons are fantastic indeed and the Uranus Beings set their own difficult challenges in the Soulforce Pool in order to gain Walker status.

MINERVA

Minerva General Reading

Minervan people are not only dreamers, they are Dreamweavers. If they are exhausted during the day, it is likely because they have been working all night long in dream or perhaps in astral states. They always feel a bit out of step on Earth and that is because they quite literally partially shift in multi dimensions. Their life energy is mutable and changes to meet the needs of what is going on around them. The lines between fantasy and reality are blurred for Minervans and if psychologists try to pigeonhole these individuals to make that a negative thing, the psychologists don't have a clue what these people go through day to day. They are natural remote viewers and can empathize with people because they have the ability, if well balanced, to "walk" in to anyone or anything. There are some cosmic rules to consider, such as how to travel safely astrally, and that "walking in" another living entity is not polite without permission. Imagine telling your child who observes that the old man's feet hurt, "It's not polite to walk in their bodies, honey, unless you have permission." Minervan people can mold dreams towards a positive conclusion, which may alter the reality of the dimension they are working in. In all probability, it isn't an actual dream. The Minervan Being can also see alternative conclusions to a set of events and "rewind" a "dream" to reset the "dream" in the right direction. Minervans have powerful possibilities to work with Spirit. In order to do so effectively, they must get more rest than most people.

Key Words: transformation; astral projection; dreamweaver; teacher; Athena.

Key Phrases: Spirit walker, can walk in other entities to view and influence.

Energy Signature: This depends where they are in the Fleur'd leis path. Any House affiliation outside of Sun or Moon or Earth is not Fleur d'leis, not training towards oneness with Spirit. Minerva is mutable Loveforce/Lifeforce depending on what is needed in the Universe.

Challenges: Obstacles to transformation; judgment of others and not self; not understanding oneness of Spirit; keeping it real when inter-dimensional and extra-dimensional lives seem real too.

Transformational Test: These beings have to pass the tests of this lifetime in order to see the Soulforce Pool again. There will be tests of the Fleur d'leis; physical, emotional, and spiritual housecleaning in this incarnation in order to achieve Fleur d'leis Transformational status to merge with the Godhead or the Soulforce Pool. These Minervans need to do Spirit's work in the Vortex system which may call for astral projection or dream intervention, weaving, interpretation or walk-in Spirit involvement.

SUN 2

Sun 2 General Reading

The face of the Sun is the face of God. We cannot gaze into the Sun without becoming blind. We cannot gaze into the true face of the Creator/God/ Sun. The intellect and consciousness of the Creator, the protector, the Father of us all, is encased in a lonely visage hidden from us all. But the Sun was born of himself in the House of Basis and he had a plan. He would share the best parts of himself with a lovely feminine mate, Diana, created out of his ideals for the best partner and the essential mother and the combination of their energies would create life on Earth and frankly other dimensions and other planets. The Creator would share another part of himself, the one everyone would know as God. This ideal God, the benevolent and loving God in a visage that could be seen and heard would keep the appearance of man and would love humankind above all of his creations. This concept of Father, Son and Holy Ghost as the triad Creator has always confused us and our explanations of the Holy Trinity have always fallen short of the truth. The Creator's form cannot be seen. The Sun is an energy that lives in us all. We are not individual beings. We are energy beings given a body in order to enjoy the physicality of Earthly life. In truth, our energy melds into one another in a dimensional extension of the Soulforce Pool in seemingly independent and autonomous form, but truly we are all part of each other and melded into one. We are beautiful beings of light and color and that is the soul and how Spirit sees us, so what think we see when we look in a mirror is not what we really are.

Key Words: Godhead; Spiritual Pool; I am; the Light; Protection.

Key Phrases: Direct spiritual influence; Lifeforce teaching; the understanding; the basis for all spiritual teaching directly from Creator; ability to see truth through anything.

Challenges: Force of least resistance.

Transformational Test: Face the Sun 2 Transformational Test as indicated by Planet in the Houses. Spirit will communicate with individuals in Sun 1 and Sun 2 placements, so this test is to become sufficiently balanced and aware in order to hear. It may also be a test of opening up to avenues and tools available to help.

MOON 2

Moon 2 General Reading

The Sun is the underlying energy for the Moon. In many mythologies, the Sun and the Moon were mates. As so often happens in long-standing relationships, the Sun became restless in the home he had made with the goddess of the Moon, Diana, in Olympus. As the Creator in the form of Zeus, the Sun had made the perfect woman who would love him without question or judgment. The trade off for such devotion, however, was a promise never to lie to her. He didn't promise faithfulness, however, and was not, by any stretch of the imagination, faithful. Diana did not judge him and remained faithful herself, but her pain at being left behind and left alone became unbearable. When Zeus, the Sun, offered to take her along in his journeys if she would only give up the warm and loving home she had created for him in Olympus, she found that she could not. Therefore he charged her with the task of handling the transformational transitions between lives and gave her dominion over the Earth and the Moon. In this Moon 2 placement, the loving Moon people are also given a great task. They must learn love and understand loss. They must consider the highest good and do whatever is necessary to achieve it. This is a lesson universal in scope and sometimes it involves leaving home when that is the last thing Moon people want to do. Travel rounds out an individual and expands the scope of their understanding of other cultures and people. In the case of Moon 2 people who must travel, it does something else. It opens the Third

Eye to a wider perspective of the needs not only of humanity, but also of the Earth itself, as well as the universal need for healing with love. Moon 2 people are tasked to actively direct this power of love universally.

Key Words: Changeable; Mother; mother influence; teacher; natural rhythms; natural inclinations. Huntress Diana, Diana of Ephesus

Key Phrases: Attitude towards the Earth and motherhood in general; way of raising children; way of looking at nurturing; way of healing, mother of us all (Diana of Ephesus multiple breasted)

Energy Signature: Loveforce/Lifeforce

Challenges: Spending habits, financial challenges

Transformational Test: These people must learn to live within their budget and let go of the material pleasures and some of the comforts in order to transform.

These people must be balanced male to female and Elementally. They must serve others and put others first. Love has to be tempered with strength of a different kind: parental consistency and tough love when necessary; and standing strong in the possibility of rejection. This is a very hard test for the loving Moon people.

EARTH /VENUS 2

Earth 2

General Reading for Earth 2

Mother Earth is alive, but not doing very well. We are polluting her skies and her water and disturbing magnetic forces of the ley-lines by irresponsible fracking and over-mining of minerals. Minerals and metals are placed where they are supposed to be in order to keep the energy of the Earth flowing. They also help the Earth receive energy from the Sun and other Planets as well as give energy reciprocally to keep our solar system in orbit. Yes, we have a big problem and although the world didn't end in December 2012, we may have only bought ourselves a short period of time before the Earth can no longer sustain life. The seas are being polluted and the marine animals who lend their energy to healing the oceans are being overfished and poisoned. Nobody wants to hear this, but it is the critically important job of Earth people to advocate for Mother Earth and to stand up for her. Earth/Venus people need to be actively working on healing the Earth and the seas and work to undo blockages in the Earth's ley-lines, sending healing where it is needed. A mother must protect her young. In order to help Mother Earth protect *our* young, Earth/Venus1 people must first protect her.

Key Words: Grounding; home values; balance; individuality.

Key Phrases: Way of looking at Earth's needs and meeting Earth's needs; way of seeing self integral to family; Way of mothering; attitude toward Earth changes and weather changes; attention to detail; healing self and others; advocate of the innocents.

Energy Signature: Lifeforce/Loveforce and Loveforce/Lifeforce.

Challenges: Self destruction; depression; almost comatose behavior when overwhelmed.

Transformational Test: These people must advocate for others who are being abused, even when those people won't advocate for themselves. These people must place the well-being of innocents above that of the accepted status quo and this may require that they are unpopular and uncomfortable in their jobs or even in their own families.

Venus 2
General Reading for Venus 2

Keep in mind that Venuvians provide the training ground between lives and help the souls shift after death into another incarnation if there are still lessons to be learned or into the Soulforce Pool if reincarnation is no longer necessary. The test of true love is the willingness to sacrifice for another. Loveforce lessons always involve a test of the willingness to sacrifice and the reason is simple. Despite the belief by some that we were instructed by God to turn the other cheek, this "instruction" was taken out of context and has been misinterpreted by various religions and sects throughout time as an excuse for people not to stand up for themselves or for others who are being persecuted. Loving people who would stand by and see a child injured and do nothing, or who see their families killed and not fight back are actually not doing God's will. God would never tell anyone not to protect themselves or their children. This book doesn't normally take on religious myths, but this is one the interpreters of the Bible really got wrong. People may not sit on a fence when something wrong is being done to them or harm is coming to them, PERIOD. Venus beings understand this and they must put themselves in harm's way, if necessary, to protect the underdog. They are expected to act, regardless of consequence to themselves, to the point of fighting back verbally or using mediation or legal channels against inhumane, illegal, bullying, or demeaning behavior. People can always try to mediate less severe problems and work things out first, but if running isn't an option when someone raises a fist or breaks out a gun, they must be prepared to fight back.

Key Words: Advocate; protector; self-sacrifice; responsible, selfless

Key Phrases: Adult love; mature self-perception; female side of Janus; male and female; Aphrodite

Energy Signature: Loveforce; the highest Loveforce. Venus' energy is combined with Earth or the Sun for balance to Lifeforce, but Venus earned Loveforce only status, by their willingness to stand up for another. Venus is the only planet with earned increment Loveforce only.

Challenges: If these people sit on a fence and won't fight for others, they haven't learned the lesson of true love; they must work to understand the duality of male and female.

Transformational Test: Self-sacrifice for others; Protection of others; Helping others to face and understand the harder aspects of love, as in tough love and the ability to give it. These people will be receiving dream training to help souls to shift from Earth 1 levels to Transformational 2 levels as well as help the souls back to the Soulforce Pool. Venus provides a resting place between lives and helps souls with their Life Path decisions for the next incarnation.

Mercury
Mercury General Reading
Mercury is just one persona of a God created by the Sun, Wellspring Father. Wellspring Father, the name used here for the Creator, took all the best parts of himself and created a clone. The capacity for joy,

love, and brotherhood, plus all the administrative qualities necessary for running a Universe, was built into his best friend, clone, and confidant, Adonis. Wellspring Father was weary of responsibility for his creations but had to make sure they were cared for. Adonis was given that responsibility for their care. Adonis has had many names: Apollo, God, Prime, and Spero Zezas (a name he used on an Earth visit that stuck); but Mercury, the messenger, was also one of his personas.

To be responsible for the Universe is a big job, especially when you have to balance, universally, the two energies of Loveforce and Lifeforce. For this, Adonis was given free rein to do whatever he needed to do. Over the centuries, it was apparent that Loveforce alone corrupted itself: it became either too selfish to sacrifice oneself for another and share their energies, or too literal in the "Thou shall not kill" area. If an innocent is being harmed, it is intrinsically necessary to protect the innocent by fighting whoever is doing the harm, and if necessary, killing them. Certainly, one cannot stand by and do nothing when an innocent is being harmed, but that is essentially what happened in the Universe with pure Loveforce with one exception: Venus Beings understood that love meant protecting others even with their lives.

So the solution was to merge the energies to balance Loveforce with Lifeforce and a universal dance ensued to mingle the energies. It really wasn't easy to do as the Planets were, at one time, divided Loveforce and Lifeforce. So all of life had to change and that change came about in 1994 with the Jupiter comet. If the planets had not accepted the basic energy change, life in the Universe would have ended instead of the comet breaking up on Jupiter. If it had hit in one place, it would have knocked Jupiter out of its orbit and that would have knocked the other planets in our solar system out of kilter, resulting in the end of life on planet Earth. Luckily, the planets all got into line with accepting a change in their energies; all except Jupiter.

Key Words: Traveler; adventurer; fluidity; student; searcher; dreamer; day-dreamer; visionary; Apollo, Adonis, Mercury.

Key Phrases: Spiritual traveler who may be called upon for spirit quest; Metaphysical and/or spiritual student, Apollo is the son of Diana and the Sun.

Energy Signature: Lifeforce/Loveforce.

Challenges: Escapism.

Transformational Test: This is the point of spherical contact, the point at which Spirit and the Earthly plane interact to help the individual move in any direction or be guided in a specific direction. How open are these people to Spirit's call to help? How open are these people to listening to an inner voice? How far will these people go to keep from hearing the inner voice? The Mercurian has to be open and balanced Elementally and male to female to receive Dream-teaching.

Quick House Guide

The Planets shown are the underlying influences. If you want to learn to do readings on your own, It is important to weigh the Planet's Energy Signature into the House dynamics and the reading as a whole. Look at the Key Energy as a key to how the individuals react. The first force energy is how they react first. If unbalanced in the Lifeforce/Loveforce (Head and Heart) energies, watch for the area that needs the most work. Combine the total energies of Lifeforce to Loveforce in the Planets and the Houses to get the final key.

THE FIRST HOUSE OF BASIS

The First House is the base line of your personality, and the foundation of the plan you set for yourself in this incarnation. It is the first house of the new incarnation you have created in your new Life Script. It is the core of your life and the foundation upon which you will build your life. The First House of Basis Chart 1 represents the Sun's birth signs. This is important, because it will help you to understand the personality of the Creator. If you share the Sun in the House of Basis as your Soulpath, you have personality traits in common with the Creator, and you are blessed. Whichever Planet you find in the First House of Basis as your Soulpath or in your draws, be aware that you have personal guidance from that Planet, as well as the underlying energy of the other Planetary teachers. Every Planet that guides the Houses has the Creator and Soulforce Pool as back up and support, and in fact, they all work in conjunction with the other Planetary energies to help guide you.

Underlying influence: Sun: Godhead; Spiritual Pool; I am; The Light.

Key Energy: Lifeforce/Lifeforce, Loveforce/Loveforce.

THE SECOND HOUSE OF VALUES

The Second House of Values covers a great many aspects of your life. It reflects your true attitude towards what you value: money and finances; home and décor; possessions and material goods; children and how to raise them; partnership dynamics; and your attitude and viewpoint toward not only your own personal appearance, but also the personal appearance of others.

Underlying influence: Moon: Changeable; Mother; mother influence; teacher; natural rhythms; natural inclinations.

Energy Signature: Loveforce/Lifeforce (always that)

THE THIRD HOUSE OF THE CONSCIOUS MIND

The Third House of the Conscious Mind is the public face, the part of your personality that you share or think you reveal to the world. This is the face you show to others which may or may not reflect how you truly feel or how you are truly perceived by others. It reflects the things you think you have control of and it reflects the personal expectations and goals you set for yourself. This House holds up a mirror to reveal not only your self-perception (how you expect yourself to react and what you think you feel) but also what others may actually see and think about you.

Underlying Planetary Influence: Equally shared by Earth/Venus:

Earth: Grounding; home values; balance between male and female energies; individuality.

Key Energy/Earth: Lifeforce/Loveforce and Loveforce/Lifeforce.

Venus: Advocate, responsible, adult love; mature self perception; female side of Janus both male and female.

Key energy/Venus: Loveforce, the highest Loveforce.

THE FOURTH HOUSE OF THE SUBCONSCIOUS MIND

The Fourth House of Subconscious Mind reveals that our perception and grasp of reality may not be what we think. It is overbalanced in Lifeforce energy for a purpose: it looks objectively at that which is hidden, and uncovers underlying motivational forces, urges, and dreams. It delves into our Dreamwork, and explores possible programming from Spirit, which requires that some kind of lesson be learned or that some response from Spirit be recognized. This House helps us to look at what may motivate us beyond normal expectations; what may be the underlying problems and challenges we experience. Mars is the teacher here, and reality checks and Lifeforce lessons are the modus operandi behind the House of the Subconscious Mind.

Underlying Planetary Influence: Mars: Aggression; war-like; warrior; tenacious.
Key Energy: Lifeforce/Lifeforce, Lifeforce/Loveforce. Note: not balanced to Loveforce.

THE FIFTH HOUSE OF THE LOVE ASPECT

The Fifth House of Love Aspect shows our attitude towards love. It is overbalanced in the Loveforce energy to emphasize our ability to love and respect ourselves as well as work on our ability to extend love to others. It shows not only our expectations about love in our lives and what we expect of others, but also what our ideal of love is, and what we will or will not do for love. It not only addresses self-love, love for someone else, but it also addresses the higher ideal of Universal love.

Underlying Planetary Influence: Neptune; Insecurity; self-love; individualist; rebel; maintenance levels.
Key Energy: Loveforce/Loveforce, Loveforce/Lifeforce. Note: not balanced in Lifeforce.

THE SIXTH HOUSE OF PHYSICAL ASPECT

The Sixth House of Physical Aspect projects your physical self-perception. This House helps you to understand how you view yourself, and seeks to build self-esteem, but it also holds a mirror up to the world of your self-perception. Your personal perspective of your physical appearance and how well you apply your strength and drive towards self-actualization is reflected in your manner of dress and the respect you show your body. The confidence and traits you portray are hopefully apparent in how you see yourself and the way you expect others to see you.

Underlying Planetary Influence: Saturn; Psychic ability; changeable; forever young; possibly eccentric; chameleon-like; individualistic wardrobe; complex nature; talker; raconteur.

Key Energy: four times Lifeforce/Loveforce, Loveforce/Lifeforce.

THE SEVENTH HOUSE OF EMOTIONAL ASPECTS

The Seventh House of Emotional Aspects helps us to understand which emotion is actually at work at the present time. Uranus is the Planet that teaches us how to handle heavy energy and come out of the challenge intact. The Planet Uranus' energy is inherently balanced to Lifeforce and Loveforce, so when we explore changeable emotions, we are able to look at them more objectively, and help ourselves understand what may be underlying situations and emotions. The House of Emotional Aspects also attempts to help us understand the emotions of others and not flee at the first sign of a tear, but to instead explore the humanity of appropriate emotional responses and socially acceptable behavior, helping us to meet the emotional expectations of others.

Underlying Planetary Influence: Uranus; Heavy energy; warrior; moody.

Key Energy: Twenty times Lifeforce/Lifeforce, Lifeforce/Loveforce, Loveforce/Loveforce.

THE EIGHTH HOUSE OF GENERATION

The Eighth House of Generation can be thought of as the "what is" House. It is the House that strips away the illusions of what we would like a situation to be, or what we are trying to make it, down to what the actual situation *is*, right now, in the moment. It helps us to know what the reality truly is in order to proceed with what we need to do next in this incarnation's plan for our Lifescript. Minerva is mutable energy and her purview is to help us to transform by doing what is necessary based upon where we actually are on our spiritual paths.

Underlying Planetary Influence: **Minerva;** Transformation; astral projection; dream work; dreamweaving; dream teaching; Athena.

Key Energy: Mutable Loveforce/Lifeforce, depends on where the individual is in their Spiritual Transformational Path shown primarily by the aspects Sun 2, Moon 2 and Earth/Venus 2 in the reading and weighing what it says there as well.

THE NINTH HOUSE OF REGENERATION

The Ninth House of Regeneration is your soul's big picture. It can best be described as the House of "becoming", one that reveals what you can be; what you are working towards. Of all the Houses, the 9th House clearly lights the way to your transformational path. It is what you can ascend to if you remain balanced, and do the work required in this incarnation or this Life Path, to achieve oneness with God/ the Spiritual Pool after death. It helps you to know that you're on the right or wrong track so you can adjust what you need to do. Sun 2/The Creator is guiding you every step of the way in this House.

Underlying Planetary Influence: Sun 2 Godhead; Spiritual Pool; I am: The Light; spiritual protection; direct communication there if individuals are balanced and aware so they may hear. It is also a test of the willingness of these individuals to open up to esoteric avenues of learning and using tools to help.

Key Energy: Lifeforce/Lifeforce, Loveforce/Loveforce.

THE TENTH HOUSE OF UNIVERSAL LIFEFORCE

The Tenth House of Universal Lifeforce addresses Lifeforce teaching and the application of all that you have learned up to this point. It is where you are in terms of a bigger universal picture of Lifeforce and what work remains to be done in order to transcend. The transformational place within the Universal Lifeforce is determined by the work *actually* done, not work intended to be done in this lifetime, not only on the material plane, but also through the work of the higher self. This requires the balance of male and female energies and that you have also achieved a balance in your Elemental affiliation. It assumes spiritual maturity, and exacts much harder tests for you to ascend to the Soulforce Pool. The rewards are very great for achieving your spiritual goals, but expect to be tested. Sun 2/Creator and Moon 2 are both on equal footing as your teachers and protectors, and they are betting on your success!

Underlying Planetary Influences; Sun 2 direct primary; Moon 2 shared primary.

Sun 2 Primary: Godhead; Spiritual Pool; I am; The Light; protection and guidance directly from the Godhead.

Key Energy, Sun 2: Lifeforce/Lifeforce, Loveforce/Loveforce.

Moon 2 Primary: Changeable; mother; mother influence; feminine teaching; natural rhythms; natural inclinations.

Key Energy, Moon 2: Loveforce/Lifeforce

THE ELEVENTH HOUSE OF UNIVERSAL LOVEFORCE

The Eleventh House of Universal Loveforce addresses where you are in terms of a bigger universal picture of Loveforce influence. The transformational place within the Universal Loveforce is determined by the work actually done by you in this Life Path by your material and higher self. You have passed all the tests you set for yourself in the Life Path Scripts of all your previous lifetimes in order to reach this point and Spirit now determines what remains to be done in order for you to transcend. Like Universal Lifeforce, this House requires the balance of male and female energies and the balance of Elemental energies, but it also requires the balance of Loveforce and Lifeforce. Spirit is watching over you very carefully because this may be the final test area for this lifetime, and success means that you will join the Soulforce Pool in transcendence after death. You may certainly expect harder tests and they will come from a formidable trio: Moon 2, Earth 2 and Venus 2. They want you to succeed, but it won't be easy!

Key Energies: Moon 2 direct primary, Earth/Venus 2 indirect)

Moon 2: Changeable; mother; mother influence; feminine influence; feminine side; natural rhythms; natural inclinations.

Key energy Moon 2: Loveforce/Lifeforce.

Venus 2: Advocate.

Key Energy, Venus 2: The highest Loveforce. Possible sacrifice of some kind for love, must work to understand the lesson of true love. Must work to understand the duality of male and female.

Earth 2; grounding; home values; balance; individuality.

Key Energy Earth 2: Lifeforce/Loveforce and Loveforce/Lifeforce. Must work with Spirit to actively heal the Earth and other planets in our solar system.

THE TWELFTH HOUSE OF KARMA

The Twelfth House of Karma is the House of Spiritual testing under duress. In all the other Houses, you have set your own Life Script for the next incarnation. In this House, Spirit sets the Soul Script and it is pass/fail. Depending on how you fare, your decisions and resolve will show Spirit the mettle of your dedication and spiritual maturity. It shows where you truly are in terms of the Lifeforce and Loveforce lessons you have learned. It tests your commitment to a bigger universal picture. The Transformational Tests you are facing are primarily from the spiritual forces that introduce challenges and lessons to our incarnations: the Vortex, Metal Elementals, and sometimes the other Elementals. Elementals place extremely difficult challenges in our paths to test how we overcome them, but it is important to understand that we are still ultimately responsible for our choices. Our souls have already determined the costs of straying from the plan we have made in between lives for this incarnation and when wrong choices are made in the Twelfth House of Karma, the karmic cost can be high. This is the area of three-fold blessing and retribution because the souls are expected to have learned all of their lessons by the time they reach this point. Quite frankly, by the time you reach this point, you have been so thoroughly trained that it is very unlikely you will make the wrong decisions or fail to act. You've got this! Spirit and the Planet that guides the Twelfth House placement very much wants you to succeed here! **Underlying Planetary Influence:** **Mercury:** Traveler; adventurer; student; searcher; dreamer; day-dreamer; visionary; how we flow; Apollo.

Key Energy: Lifeforce/Loveforce.

Elements

Fire Element

Who is a Fire Element person? Picture in your mind a small flame that barely ignites before it rushes forward to consume whatever fuel it can find to grow, and therein lies the basis for individuals with Fire placement. Fire devours whatever is in its path that offers the least resistance to being consumed and/or illuminated. For Fire Beings, free movement and expression are often not tendered by caution in speech or action. Fire Element people are the bull in the china shop. They don't mean to be unfeeling or uncaring with regard to somebody else's emotions, or exhibit inappropriate social behavior; they don't seem to be able to constrain themselves from reacting, and that, obviously, will cause them a great deal of trouble in life.

If Fire is weak in the chart, there is a lack of joy and playfulness in life. These people may lack the energy to motivate themselves to get off the couch and turn off the TV. They may have a sluggish digestive system, limiting them to eating light because heavy or spicy foods won't digest well. Depression and a lack of self-esteem and confidence could be a problem until the Fire Element is restored. This can be accomplished by being around other fire people who have energy to spare and aren't in the "consume" mode. It can also be achieved by spending time out in the Sun, enjoying nature, or exercising.

Fire Element people have palpable energy that radiates to everyone around them. They can't sit still for very long and get bored with anything or anybody who doesn't MOVE or act on impulse. Too much fire can be a wildfire or worse, but Fire Element people should never even think about having a drink to try to settle down. What is alcohol? Fuel for hotter fire! Excess fire can only be dampered by giving energy to those who need it. When Fire energy is offered, then the other Elements of Water, Air, and Earth can reciprocally offer their energy to damper the flames. It is a nice trade off. Fire just has to be careful when giving and taking energy from others. If there are no calming individuals around to help or who need help, excess Fire can be sent off through the head chakra to the Sun or the universal Matrix. It can always be used there.

Fire in appropriate proportions warms and protects. These people are the entrepreneurs of life, anxious for new projects, and full of great ideas. They are dedicated and enthusiastic and can motivate others to "just do it!"

Colors: Red; yellow; orange, St. Michael's Fire Blue; white.
Tag Words Balanced State: Fire; Energy; passion; strong sexual identity; playfulness; ability to go with the flow; active; impulsive but aware of consequences; burning brightly with caring energy.
Tag Words Imbalanced State: Lack of fire; lack of energy; lack of passion; control issues; sexual abstinence or lack of interest in sex; lack of playfulness; anti-social; impulsive without thinking of consequences unable to go with the flow; erratic; unmotivated; aggressive; submissive; inactive; apathetic.
Health: Good digestion or poor digestion; good self-image; poor self-image; euphoric; depressed; exercises to relax; lack of exercise/ennui.
Transformation Key: When the digestion begins to regulate, the body will start to get everything else in control.
Spiritual Test/ Lifeforce Lesson: Learn a level of control that burns slowly and steadily, and the extreme highs and extreme lows will go away.
Spiritual Test/Loveforce Lesson: Learn to love yourself and think of others needs before your own. Learn to think of consequences of actions and what is being said. Do no harm.

Air–Ether Element

In traditional astrology, the Air Elementals are synonymous with those who pursue higher intellectual endeavors; the thinkers, the planners, and the dreamers of abstract thought. Their spacey demeanor is legend. All of this is true to a point, but Air Elementals are more legendary than previously understood. Air Beings exist in a half step off Earth's dimension, and so are the most likely to be attuned to the Spiritual Pool's directives for the planet's and solar system's health.

In intellectual pursuits, they are heads above the other Elementals, literally. However, they are rarely listened to. Air Beings work for the higher good of the Planet and mankind and its pursuits. I always picture the quiet one in the boardroom who remains calm in the face of the furious talking head debates. The one who quietly asks everyone to sit down and says, to the only other quiet one, "George, did you tell them your idea about how to increase sales?" The Air people don't need the podium and the praise; they just needs people to do what needs to be done to solve the problem without all of the drama and emotional backlash.

When Air People look out the window, don't assume that they aren't working. Air people get more thinking, processing, and planning done while daydreaming or smoking cigarettes on break than the average person does in a week. For some reason, many Air Beings smoke.

Air Beings can work very effectively with the public because they remain calm in the storms of verbal communication. They are the people who can cut through the emotions and the drama to quiet the ranting masses and help them solve problems. They are A-Z, step-by-step thinkers: everything has to follow what came before and what comes after has to be in probable and natural progression. As a result of A-Z thinking, Air Beings are integrally important to the success of any plan.

They can be assertive, however, and it is a Transformation Test in their lives that they eventually take a stand for themselves and others. In their own families, surprisingly enough, they are the center of their families' worlds. Their families remain close and are happy units for the most part. Air Beings are the peacekeepers and the calm in every storm, even if they marry rebellious and passionate action types. Air Beings' children will be well behaved and will be given enough freedom to find themselves. Princess clothes and capes are always an option.

Air Beings need peace in their homes and at work to function happily. They need to connect with nature and the open skies. The Transformational Test for Air Beings is to remain balanced in order to do the things they need to do for themselves that allow Spirit to help direct them in the everyday. A message to the Air Beings from Spirit is this: "Be sure to take that yoga class for you. Enlist in the college painting course you've wanted to take forever. Take a day off work and play in the sand with your children and/or grandchildren." They need people around them who value them and listen to them. Ideally, they should quit jobs that don't honor them, but realistically, they stay because they are needed most where there are problems to be solved.

Colors: White, Blue, Turquoise.
Tag Words Balanced State: Sufficient air; balance; dream-state; waking dreams; daydreams; sacrifice; harmony; joy; feeling a connection to everything and everybody; feeling a connection to the Godhead.
Tag Words Imbalanced State: Lack of air; imbalance; inability to dream; insufficient REM sleep; lack of joy; not feeling connected to anything; not feeling connected to the Godhead.
Health: Air Beings must advocate enough for themselves not to take on work that time doesn't allow to be done. If they don't, they may have problems with the throat, bowels, or nervous system and often problems with breathing, asthma, allergies, recurrent lung infections, anemia, lack of energy, and joy of life. They must find a way to leave work at work and enjoy the home and family in order to have the peace of mind they crave.
Transformation Key: Air Beings have to stay balanced to hear Spirit's directives for the everyday and do things for themselves that they enjoy without feeling guilty.
Spiritual Test: Air Element people have to be balanced sufficiently to speak up and stand up for themselves and advocate for others. They must advocate within the family for peace, no matter what the cost.

Water Element

Water Beings are sublimely in touch with their own feelings and the unspoken feelings of others. They are often thought to be psychic, but really, it is a matter more of empathy and sympathy and the ability to put themselves in the other person's shoes, seeing things from a shifting perspective. This is a wonderful ability because Water

Beings make the best friends in the world. They know when to speak and when to be silent, and they know when to stay and when to go.

Water Beings often act without really understanding their own motives because they are tuned into the flow of what is happening around them. Think about the characteristics of water. Water Beings embody all of them: It is sometimes placid and quiet, sometimes violent. Sometimes it dances to the vibrations of the Planet Earth and the Moon and sometimes it is dangerous, muddy and quick moving and terrain altering. It can transform and go from liquid to solid and crystalize in unique snow flake patterns. Water can be liquid, solid or when heated transmutes to steam. Water is affected by heat but also by cold; the movement of water is made more sluggish by cold. Water Beings too can be subtle in their movements, but inexorable. They can generally influence everything around them to bend to their will.

What Water Beings need to remember is obstacles submerged are still there, so they will eventually have to be dealt with, unless one has eons of time available to wear them down slowly. Water Beings are a group mind; they are not one of millions of little individual water babies, but part of a whole. Water people feel everything around them, and if open, they can feel the Universe as well. They have the ability to help Spirit and help heal the Universe if they want to. They just need to "tune" in.

The person in this placement has ties to the Mother, and to the feminine Moon's ebbs and flows. The Water Element is important to understand because it can teach people the most about themselves. Water Beings are fluid in thought and action, but can be changeable. Water Beings have a way of going with the flow and are ready, at the drop of a hat, to switch directions. If trapped and unable to move even by seeping deep into the aquifer, water stagnates, grows algae, and eventually reverts to Earth. In solid or liquid form, water has the power to move mountains, carve stone, extinguish fire, and can transform itself into ice or steam, regenerating back into the atmosphere as rain returning to the sea. It is changeable and magical. It has Lifeforce of an emotional Loveforce/Lifeforce nature and is sensitive to all that is around it. It flows around obstacles and can eventually wear them away or submerge them entirely.

Color: All shades of Blue and Aqua.

Tag Words Balanced State: Deep sense of going with the flow; feeling connected to other Water Beings via vibration and sound; able to be moved by music and feel healed by music.

Tag Words Imbalanced State: Inability to go with the flow; feeling suffocated; feeling like one is drowning or being oppressed by weight; inability to feel joy in sound and music.

Health: Water must keep flowing, and the body requires a great deal of water. Depriving a Water Beings of pure and clean water will affect all aspects of the body's health, creating kidney, liver, urinary, stomach, and digestive problems.

Transformation Key: Water Beings not only go with the flow in all areas of life but are within the flow and can feel Earth's energy. Water Beings need to learn balance in order to tune into the Earth Beings as well.

Spiritual Test: Water is a group mind and the Water Being must learn to work and meld with other Water Beings. Water must flow and the energy of this being must flow or it will become stagnant and the body will sicken. More importantly, the Water Beings cannot pour purified energy into the universal water structures to help Spirit heal wellspring (water) if their own energy is impure or blocked. Water can take many forms. A Water Being must be able to transmute and transform as nature requires.

Earth Element

Earth Element people are grounded, rooted, and like to be close to the Earth. They feel the power in the Earth and feel a part of a larger whole. They feel connected, and it is this connection that the other signs crave and rarely feel. At all times, they are, on some level, aware of the movements of magnetic energy and the weather. They sense wrongness with pollution and sense chakra blockages in the Earth. They rejuvenate in the mountains and the best part of going to the beach is walking in the sand. They are tied to Mother Earth, and they will make good, loving parents. Both male and females are nurturers. Earth Elementals are tied to the Moon as well and tend to be star-gazers and cloud watchers. The energy of the Moon is linked inherently to the tidal waves of the sea, the energy of the Earth, and the water in the body.

Earth people bank their feelings. They are not always easy to read, and they tend to observe the situation and process before they decide what is going on. They enjoy sensory feelings. They love to eat the things that Earth produces. They enjoy the color, texture, and taste of food and often make little humming sounds when they eat. Earth people tend to have strong family values and strong attachments to an extended family. They are affectionate and have healthy sexual interests. They like to touch people when they talk and may tend to stand closer than some other Elementals are comfortable with.

Everyone always says that Earth folk are practical and dogmatic. More accurately, they are realistic and do what needs to be done to finish the job, and then they want to go play outside. Earth people like the comfort of knowing where their stuff is and they like nice stuff. They don't like others playing with or MOVING their stuff (the ultimate sin!) They never outgrow this.

People who lack the Earth Element don't feel connected to anything. They feel like they are adrift in a sea of apathy. They don't enjoy sensory experiences and the blandness of their sensibilities is mind numbing. If as an Earth Being you experience this ennui, the remedy is to go play with the kids or bury yourself in the sand, make mud pies, or roll in the dirt with your animals. Go to the mountains to regroup and recoup. Ask for help from the Earth, and she will be glad to help you. Try to remember to help her back sometimes.

The Transformational Test for Earth Element Beings is to not only to be balanced well enough to take energy from the Earth and Sun, but also to be able to give it back as Spirit and Mother Earth require so as to move energy where it is needed. They can literally extend their Earth energy to heal and balance the other planets as well as the Earth. Earth Element people may be called upon to heal the hurts and gaps between females for sure and possibly between females and males. They are great listeners and good mediators. Because they have the gift of non-judgment, people will feel like they can tell Earth Beings anything and they can rely upon them for great advice and counsel.

Colors: Brown, brown-black, greens.

Tag Words Balanced State: Connected to Earth energy; grounded; feeling like part of a team or a whole; able to enjoy sensory pleasure; nurturing.

Tag Words Imbalanced State: Lack of Earth energy not feeling grounded; feeling isolated from the whole; unable to feel sensory pleasure; unable to nurture the self and/or others.

Health: Issues to do with the heart, love issues affecting the heart; issues with circulation; tendency to be depressed if they don't get outside to play and draw grounding from the Sun and Earth.

Transformation Key: The more balanced Earth Beings are, the more connected they are to the Earth itself, and the more energy they have.

Spiritual Test: Earth Beings must place the well being of innocents above that of the accepted status quo, that may require being unpopular and perhaps uncomfortable in their jobs or even within their own families. They must become so aware of Earth's planetary health that they can feel energy moving through her poles. Corruption will feel like wrongness along ley-lines of the Earth. Earth people must work with Spirit to actively heal the Earth, and perhaps other planets in our solar system.

Wood Element

Wood Beings give their lives for the sustenance of others, for oxygen, shade, and warmth, as well as for food or to provide materials for building homes. However, this giving is supposed to have a tradeoff. Wood Beings are supposed to be allowed to grow and thrive without having to cope with disease not caused by nature but inflicted upon them by others. They have a spiritual path in Earth's transformation as natural record keepers of their time on the planet. The largest organism on the planet is an Aspen tree colony. Aspens live a rich life, together as one; and what one suffers is felt by all others. Although they are rooted to the Earth, they are interconnected in a beautiful intricate web of life.

People born in the shade of the Wood Beings have most of the traits above. They are group organisms too. In truth, we all are interconnected light beings, but Wood Beings are aware of their connection to others. They dance to the beat of a different drummer and feel subtle changes in the Earth and weather and in those around them as if they were experiencing it themselves; and they are. They have the ability to literally walk a mile in another's shoes.

People born in the Element of Wood or influenced by it will probably keep a journal. They may have asthma or allergy symptoms and react adversely to pollutants and chemicals. They often have trouble with their lungs and their alimentary systems (bowels) must be kept clean to keep their bodies from becoming toxic. Additionally, they may have problems with stiffness, arthritis, or diseases that cause them to be immobile...to be wooden.

Wood Beings are wise beyond their years and people always tell them their troubles. They understand everything and judge rarely. They understand what is said and what is not said. They would make excellent mediators, but they will not advocate for anyone who would hurt another or hurt something innocent. A Spiritual Test for Wood Beings is to advocate for Earth and to use their substantial influence to move others to advocate for Earth. Spirit is tasking them with moving off the couch, away from the computer or television, and taking their noses out of the books in order to do the work that they must do to advocate for their leafier cousins and for the Earth. Spirit often lights a fire under their posteriors for their own good. Something will happen that will make them good and mad. Once that fire is lit, Wood Beings can be tireless and dynamic forces advocating for causes that affect us all.

Color: All shades of brown and green, yellow, orange, red.

Tag Words Balanced State: Feeling grounded in a different way than the Earth person, as a part of nature rather than as a visitor seeking to be soothed or regenerated by returning to nature; contributing to the healing of the Earth by working with the beings who pollinate and provide sustenance, including the faery realm and woodland creatures; having the ability to draw a great deal of energy from the Sun; having a sense of the magical everywhere and the ability to see forms in clouds and grasses and trees; having the ability to act on thoughts.

Tag Words Imbalanced State: Feeling stuck and immoveable; unable to access the energies of faery and woodland; unable to sense magic; living in the head instead of acting on thoughts.

Health: Wood requires water. There is a tendency to suffer stiffness of joints, arthritis, and perhaps diseases that result in immobility.

Transformation Key: Not to be stuck in place but learn to lean into the wind instead of fighting it and risking harm.

Spiritual Test: Spirit requires Wood Beings to make themselves mobile when their tendency is to live in one place, doing the same thing day after day. It is not a natural tendency for Wood Beings to move, but move they must.

Metal Element

Imagine giving a ball of tangled strands of necklaces to someone who can untangle the knots and interweaving almost magically, as if it were the easiest thing in the world: this is a Metal Element person. Metal in the Universe has a structure similar to a stacked DNA strand viewed from above, or a spider web of weaving and cocooning that surrounds everything: the minute cells that make up our bodies, the planets, the solar system, and the Universe as a whole. On some level, and certainly in their higher-self level, Metal Element people are keenly aware of this matrix, micro-small and infinite. If they are sufficiently balanced, they work on it nightly.

Metal Beings are traditionally thought of as being cold and unfeeling. This is not entirely true. They are naïve. They are children in their approach to loving one another. Their curiosity comes from a mental objectivity, and this drives them to try to dissect and probe the tender feelings that they and others feel. They are just trying to understand, in a cerebral, almost alien way, what is not head-oriented, but heart-oriented. When Metal Element people decide they love you, they really love you, and it is wonderful and magical to be on the recipient side of that love.

When Metal Element Beings have their first child, they don't inherently love that child the second they see him or her. They have to get to know their offspring better. Eventually their love will be an all-encompassing love, but in the beginning, their child is essentially only a creature that is shorter and more helpless than they are. Helpless beings are confusing. Metal Beings will work with the child to develop intellectual prowess from the get-go and will delight in every success and new achievement. Wait until the child can pour water or sand from receptacle to receptacle! The Metal Element parents will happily watch their little one do that for hours.

The ultimate Spiritual Test for Metal Being is finding love.

Color: Metallic luster of all shades.

Tag Words for Balanced State: Balanced toward Lifeforce for strength and objectivity; strength, connectivity to a whole; ability to sense pathways and the fibers that run across the Universe in a spider web fashion connecting planets, suns, and galaxies; the ability to envision or create energy "cocoons" or meshes of protection; feeling connected and a part of a very big universal picture; the ability to connect to reality and draw clear lines between fantasy/reality; vivid or prophetic dreams; being aware that dream lessons are being received; learning and building on dream lessons; dream re-working to create positive, life affirming and correct solutions; ability to love and extend love to others; ability to enjoy sensual and sexual pleasures.

Tag Words for Imbalanced State: Gaps in connectivity; inability to sense universal pathways; inability to envision or create energy "cocoons" or meshes of protection; feeling disconnected and intensely alone; feeling disconnected from reality; fantasy/reality lines unclear; bad dreams; being unaware that dream lessons are being received and not learning the lessons; inability to direct the dreams to desired or alternative solutions; inability to fully love and extend love to others; inability to enjoy sensual and sexual pleasures.

Health: Watch circulation; poor circulation due to interrupted ley-lines of the body and blockages; watch carbs; low carbohydrate diet is important to Metal Beings; watch weight gain; exercise vital.

Transformation Key: Practice control in dreams; ability to re-wind the dream and affect the outcome of bad dreams; creative visualization for alternative realities.

Lifeforce Spiritual Test: Work with the Vortex and Metal Elementals mending the chakras and matrix of the Universe; Vortex teaching.

Loveforce Spiritual Test: Bigger test: learning to love.

Emphasis Cards

Physical

The Physical body. Concerns about health and healthy lifestyle. Consider that in order to be healthy, physical exercise and healthy eating and lifestyles must be a part of daily living. It may be time to re-evaluate where your time is spent and determine if it is being spent wisely.*

Emotional

The Emotional Aspects. How emotions are playing into the scenario. Try to look at things more objectively and from another's viewpoint. If understanding which emotion is coming into play and not knowing and not understanding is an issue, ask for help from Spirit. *

Spiritual

Spiritual Health. How healthy is this viewpoint in terms of spiritual growth? Weigh what is easy against what is right for the answer. Do the hard things but if that answer is too complicated and needlessly hurting someone else is inevitable, ask for help in dreamtime from Spirit. Ask for other alternatives.*

*For more detailed information, see the Physical, Emotional, and Spiritual Hand Charts in *Spirit Speaks-The Transformation Connection* by Johan Adkins

Divinity Cards

The Divinity Cards are six cards that can be used alone or as a double check or worked with in conjunction New Spirit Astrology System draws to answer specific questions. Again, use the "threefold request" or state "I ask this question, the perfect way, the perfect number of times." Use these cards and store them in this order.

Card 1	Yes
Card 2	No
Card 3	I don't know or I can't answer
Card 4	Regroup the cards, cleanse, and try later
Card 5	It is not to your highest good to answer at this time
Card 6	Rephrase your question and focus

Remember not to ask two questions in one and to use "computer logic." If you say, for example, "Can you tell me if Bill likes me?" You have asked a confusing question. It might say "yes." Yes doesn't mean Bill likes you; it means "Yes, I can tell you." But in this case you should not abuse the cards by asking about a third person unless Bill is sitting beside you, and indicates his approval to ask.

If the response, "It is not to your highest good to answer at this time" is drawn, be assured that the answer was given and it will be revealed at the proper time to your spiritual development. Think of it like a data dump in REM memory. The answer is there to be retrieved when you are more ready to hear it.

Blank Cards

There are six Blank Cards which can either be included in your New Spirit Astrology System deck shuffle or not. If a Blank Card is drawn for a Planetary, House, Elemental, Emphasis, or Divinity Card in a reading, the area where it is drawn does not play strongly into the reading and the rest of the draws should be read as drawn. You could draw again, but a more true reading will be had from the initial drawing.

For instance, you combine all of the cards and draw three cards. You get a Planetary Card, a Blank Card and an Elemental Card. You would only read the two... the Planetary Card and the Elemental Card. If you doubt the draw, work with your Divinity Cards to check out the verity.

The Blank Cards are used as separation for the natural order of the deck. However, you may choose to assign any positive value to the Blank Cards based upon your own design. Just do a threefold blessing over the card and ask that it be included with the Divinity Cards and that it represent, for example, "Relationship." Mark a specific card and store it in the future with your Divinity section. I would caution you against assigning any negative value or wording to your blanks so that you do not negate the power of the deck by allowing negative influences to infiltrate it.

Quick Guides for Fast Reference

The Little White Book of New Spirit Astrology by Johan Adkins

Sun 1	1		2		3		4	
Moon 1	2		3		4		5	
Earth /Venus 1	3		4		5		6	
Mars	4		5		6		7	
Neptune	5		6		7		8	
Saturn	6		7		8		9	
Uranus	7		8		9		10	
Minerva	8		9		10		11	
Sun 2	9		10		11		12	
Moon 2	10		11		12		1	
Earth /Venus2	11		12		1		2	
Mercury	12		1		2		3	

Sun 1	5		6		7		8	
Moon 1	6		7		8		9	
Earth/ Venus 1	7		8		9		10	
Mars	8		9		10		11	
Neptune	9		10		11		12	
Saturn	10		11		12		1	
Uranus	11		12		1		2	
Minerva	12		1		2		3	
Sun 2	1		2		3		4	
Moon 2	2		3		4		5	
Earth/ Venus2	3		4		5		6	
Mercury	4		5		6		7	

Sun 1	9	10	11	12
Moon 1	10	11	12	1
Earth/Venus 1	11	12	1	2
Mars	12	1	2	3
Neptune	1	2	3	4
Saturn	2	3	4	5
Uranus	3	4	5	6
Minerva	4	5	6	7
Sun 2	5	6	7	8
Moon 2	6	7	8	9
Earth/Venus2	7	8	9	10
Mercury	8	9	10	11

REFERENCE GUIDE FULL CHARTS

BASIS CHART 1

House	Planet
1	Sun 1
2	Moon 1
3	Earth/Venus 1
4	Mars
5	Neptune
6	Saturn
7	Uranus
8	Minerva
9	Sun 2
10	Moon 2
11	Earth/Venus 2
12	Mercury

VALUES CHART 2

House	Planet
2	Sun 1
3	Moon 1
4	Earth/Venus 1
5	Mars
6	Neptune
7	Saturn
8	Uranus
9	Minerva
10	Sun 2
11	Moon 2
12	Earth/Venus 2
1	Mercury

CONSCIOUS MIND CHART 3

House	Planet
3	Sun 1
4	Moon 1
5	Earth/Venus 1
6	Mars
7	Neptune
8	Saturn
9	Uranus
10	Minerva
11	Sun 2
12	Moon 2
1	Earth/Venus 2
2	Mercury

SUBCONSCIOUS MIND CHART 4

House	Planet
4	Sun 1
5	Moon 1
6	Earth/Venus 1
7	Mars
8	Neptune
9	Saturn
10	Uranus
11	Minerva
12	Sun 2
1	Moon 2
2	Earth/Venus 2
3	Mercury

LOVE ASPECT CHART 5

House	Planet
5	Sun 1
6	Moon 1
7	Earth/Venus 1
8	Mars
9	Neptune
10	Saturn
11	Uranus
12	Minerva
1	Sun 2
2	Moon 2
3	Earth/Venus 2
4	Mercury

PHYSICAL ASPECT CHART 6

House	Planet
6	Sun 1
7	Moon 1
8	Earth/Venus 1
9	Mars
10	Neptune
11	Saturn
12	Uranus
1	Minerva
2	Sun 2
3	Moon 2
4	Earth/Venus 2
5	Mercury

EMOTIONAL ASPECT CHART 7

House	Planet
7	Sun 1
8	Moon 1
9	Earth/Venus 1
10	Mars
11	Neptune
12	Saturn
1	Uranus
2	Minerva
3	Sun 2
4	Moon 2
5	Earth/Venus 2
6	Mercury

GENERATION CHART 8

House	Planet
8	Sun 1
9	Moon 1
10	Earth/Venus 1
11	Mars
12	Neptune
1	Saturn
2	Uranus
3	Minerva
4	Sun 2
5	Moon 2
6	Earth/Venus 2
7	Mercury

REGENERATION CHART 9

House	Planet
9	Sun 1
10	Moon 1
11	Earth/Venus 1
12	Mars
1	Neptune
2	Saturn
3	Uranus
4	Minerva
5	Sun 2
6	Moon 2
7	Earth/Venus 2
8	Mercury

UNIVERSAL LIFEFORCE CHART 10

House	Planet
10	Sun 1
11	Moon 1
12	Earth/Venus 1
1	Mars
2	Neptune
3	Saturn
4	Uranus
5	Minerva
6	Sun 2
7	Moon 2
8	Earth/Venus 2
9	Mercury

UNIVERSAL LOVEFORCE CHART 11

House	Planet
11	Sun 1
12	Moon 1
1	Earth/Venus 1
2	Mars
3	Neptune
4	Saturn
5	Uranus
6	Minerva
7	Sun 2
8	Moon 2
9	Earth/Venus 2
10	Mercury

KARMA CHART 12

House	Planet
12	Sun 1
1	Moon 1
2	Earth/Venus 1
3	Mars
4	Neptune
5	Saturn
6	Uranus
7	Minerva
8	Sun 2
9	Moon 2
10	Earth/Venus 2
11	Mercury

CONDENSED ASPECT SORT BY HOUSE FOR EASE OF REFERENCE
(SEE THE WEBSITE FOR ASPECT SORT BY PLANET)

1st House of Basis

Sun 1 in the 1st House of Basis: These people are beloved of Spirit and blessed throughout their lifetimes with direct communication with the Creator and all his creations. If they remain balanced, open, and receptive, they will hear direct guidance from above. They must work hard to fulfill Spirit's directives. The harder they try, successful or not, the greater the happiness afforded in this blessed existence.

Moon 1 in the 1st House of Basis: The energy of the Moon as Loveforce and the underlying energy of the Sun as Lifeforce is in perfect balance in this placement. These people will have the energy to create and will feel inspired to do so. They have the perfect opportunity with this solid base to accomplish anything they desire as long as they stay balanced. They can expect to have guidance to do what is right. If they are imbalanced male to female and/or elementally, they must guard against the ability to "hear" guidance to do what is wrong. With this placement of power, negative influences are drawn to try to influence and confuse the issues. It would be advisable for the Moon people to be aware and surround themselves with love and light, using the threefold protection mantra, "I will hear only that which is of pure heart and love and light. I close my perception and my hearing to that which is not pure of heart." Mantras of communication with Spirit need to be repeated three times: once to state the intention, once to get the attention of Spirit, and once to seal the intention.

Earth/Venus 1 in the 1st House of Basis: These people will be tested for how deeply they can love unconditionally. The deepest teaching for these people will be to learn that Loveforce alone is not enough because it is ultimately self-serving. Spirit's message is very clear: care enough about yourself and others not to accept harm or abuse. On a more positive note, these people will act as peacemakers and hold their families together with gluey love. They are best suited to teaching a loving aspect to others. They will be the one relied upon in a crisis to always be the loving hands and the caring individuals. Their love is deep and abiding.

Mars in the 1st House of Basis: These people have been warriors in most of their lifetimes and even in this one, they will experience their fair share of troubles with mates, children, and immediate family. For the most part, Mars Beings aren't fully understood. They do what they need to do to survive, and get along as best they can. If they are forced to hold their tongue to accommodate someone else's needs, they will probably not be able to deal with the situation as rationally as they would have if the problem had just been hashed out when it first arose. On the other hand, they can be good friends to a few people, and that's the way they like it. They must be nurtured in order to love, and they do need to love.

Neptune in the 1st House of Basis: The House of Basis has, at its center, the energy of the Sun or Godhead, teaching, guiding, and sometimes confusing the Neptunian aspects. What you have operating here are the quintessential polar opposites of the Universe, Lifeforce and Loveforce, working at odds in setting up the groundwork for these individuals. Neptune is always love-based first, and in this House, there is a sharing of heart and mind. Neptune's cold aloofness melts in the Sun. This creates not only people with deep and abiding love but also people who are warm, friendly, and comfortable in their own skin. It is true that Neptunians might have a sardonic sense of humor as a result of the Sun's influence, but it will all be in good, albeit strange, and a little kinky, fun.

Saturn in the 1st House of Basis: These folks are naturally light and bright, and adding the underlying Sun's energy just makes them more so. The reason is that Lifeforce and Loveforce are amplified here, but balanced well, so that with just the smallest amount of effort, these individuals may stay eternally balanced. As such, these beings are happy, well adjusted, and larger than life. If you are attempting to raise consciousness, this is the perfect placement for it if you are balanced. If you are unbalanced (and you will know this by either being basically happy and at peace, or not), a different energy is at work here. To fix this, all you have to do is stop the negative thinking and speaking, and stop whatever you are doing to pollute your body. It won't take long to go in the right direction and for the positive and life-affirming forces to return to you. Be strong, avoid the junk food aisles, and eat your fruits and vegetables.

Uranus in the 1st House of Basis: Life will make more sense and will be less dramatic if you can just train yourself to trust your gut instincts because spiritual help will stream from the navel chakra in this instance. The Sun's underlying influence here is a test of your mettle: can you handle the situation like a mature adult would and should? Don't accept bad manners or poor demeaning behavior without speaking out. It can be done diplomatically without punching an offender in the nose because your stomach will warn you, and the Sun/Godhead is there whispering in your ear, telling you how to proceed. You must stay balanced, or that stomach warning may result in an ulcer when you don't act.

Minerva in the 1st House of Basis: All psychic abilities and ability to work with Spirit in the dreamstate will be enhanced in this aspect. You won't have vague whisperings or half feelings that you are gifted as something more in this life. You will know it without any question. If you are happy, balanced, and take care of your body, exercise, and eat right, a whole new world is about to open up for you. A key to staying balanced is to make sure you get more rest than usual. Your higher-self will be going to night school, and upon graduation, you will have earned mental clarity and a rich spiritual connection. If you don't allow for the extra hours of night school, you'll be too weary to stay balanced. Catch 22.

Sun 2 in the 1st House of Basis: Sun 2 energy gives spiritual direction straight from the Creator. Like Sun 1, these beings have the ability to work with energy and light to heal anything from a cell to a Universe. However, unlike Sun 1, they are expected to be actively doing this work. Spirit is speaking to them and requesting their help. It is probable that they hear voices, and those voices can be quite insistent about what help is needed. This help can take the form of lending a hand to a stranger or being awakened in the middle of the night by a bell ringing, a non-existent phone ringing, or knocking heard at the door when nobody is there. These are common signals to wake up and listen to Spirit.

Moon 2 in the 1st House of Basis: Moon 2 energy is Loveforce and the underlying energy of Sun 2 is Lifeforce, and the perfect balance of power between these two energies is constantly in flux among all combinations of Planets and Houses in relation to each other. If Moon 2 people are imbalanced, they will not only hear negative direction, but they may be attacked. In this placement, these Moon 2 people must learn metaphysical defense methods.*   On a brighter note, there is so much energy to do good things here, that life will be full and happy, blessed as it is with the protection of the Creator. Direct dialogue with the Creator is possible with this placement.

Earth/Venus 2 in the 1st House of Basis: Loveforce is the basis for Venus energy and the personality in this placement, but the key to these people's own well-balanced spirituality is to temper love with Lifeforce, the basis of the natural planet of this placement, the Sun. They will be tested regarding how deeply they can love unconditionally. Spirit's message is very clear; care enough about yourselves and others not to accept harm or abuse. On a more positive note, these people will hold their families together with love, and they will be the ones who can always be relied upon in a crisis. Their love is deep and abiding.

Mercury in the 1st House of Basis: Mercury Beings have a very rich and comprehensive dream life. If they can manage to be balanced, they will be receiving instruction directly from their dreams. Mercury Beings have affiliations to Metal and like their namesake Mercury, they are fluid, flowing, and changeable. These people have big responsibilities to Spirit to be messengers, and because they don't really like having to be responsible to anyone, not even to Spirit, they must perhaps spend some time on a spiritual journey or quest to help themselves come to terms with what they must be willing to do.

2nd House of Values

Sun 1 in the 2nd House of Value: An important life lesson for the Sun in the House of Values people is to pick their battles and prioritize what is truly important to them, learning to let others have their way sometimes. A Spiritual Lesson here is to learn to listen and work on grace and control issues. Sun Beings crave harmony and balance; however, they instigate matters constantly that cause disharmony. Their Spiritual Test is to learn to value the opinions and feelings of others by practicing complete silence and learning to listen without feeling the need to fix everything and everybody.

Moon 1 in the 2nd House of Value: These people will have difficulty holding onto money because buy for the pleasure of buying and giving. The real secret is that they don't like things to stay the same. They are inclined to gamble and take chances financially. In all probability, they will make and lose several fortunes in their lifetimes. The Spiritual Test for them, however, is to get their spiritual priorities in line and learn to value family and self first. They must begin to practice a "give-away" mentality. The priority is to gather people together, not things.

Earth/Venus 1 in the 2nd House of Value: The Spiritual Test for Earth/Venus 1 people in the House of Values will be tough. At some point in their lives, they will need to figure out why they give and how they can shift their values away from possessions. The Spiritual Test for the Earth/Venus 1 in the House of Values, will be to restructure your life to live within your means, budget, and plan for emergencies. When the symbiotic energy of the kundalini rises, generally during the forties or fifties, a shift in spiritual perception will ensue. This shift prompts these individuals to do a physical, emotional, and spiritual housecleaning as well as an actual physical house cleaning. They will need to part with things in order to move out from under a suffocating feeling. When the excess is cleared and cleaned away, the suffocating feelings will be too.

Mars in the 2nd House of Values: Mars Beings are the ones whom everyone will remember loving and hating. They will always have to watch that warlike tendencies don't wound inappropriately, and will need to curb the need to lash out, saying what might be hurtful. There are likely to be problems relating to women and mother figures in this aspect. Mars can exert an intimidating influence on others. The saving grace is that Moon's underlying influence puts love first. If tough love is needed, the strength to give it is here. Teachers born here are a tough nut, but they are the ones who will be able to handle the rougher students and problems that send others away screaming.

Neptune in the 2nd House of Values: Neptunes in this place won't be easily understood. They will observe the object of their affection for some time before they decide to commit themselves, even in a small way. Neptune Beings will be loving, attentive, and interested in everything, but in the back of their minds, they are like deer in the headlights, looking for reasons to run. They are also looking for reasons to trust that if they are their true selves, they will still be loved. The same processing takes place with major financial decisions they have to make. Any major expenditure of cash will happen only slowly and methodically. These beings aren't stingy, and they aren't afraid to spend where they choose to spend it; they just have to think about it first, and decide what they want the most. Neptune people are firm and strict parents who will tend to show their love by doing things with their children, and taking the time to teach them things.

Saturn in the 2nd House of Values: This will be a fun household, dramatic and larger than life, with plays in the dining room after supper starring the family dog as the dragon; pure fantasy on parade! Even though these changeable Saturnians may be just one step away from financial disaster, they will keep life interesting for their freedom-loving families, and the ride will definitely be worth it. There is so much love in this household where everyone talks at once but every voice is heard. It is very unlikely that this family will raise juvenile delinquents. The children will be extremely well adjusted, albeit a little different than their "normal" friends. But what's normal anyway?

Uranus in the 2nd House of Values: Uranus Beings are, in many ways, very young souls here, and as a result, they can be materially single minded and stubborn in their drive to get what they want when they want it, and determined to get their way. If Uranians are single, then they may find themselves with ridiculous toys, and in financial difficulty due to self-indulgence, but if Uranus Beings are mated, an "I deserve this" attitude will not be appreciated by their partners. The Transformational Test here is for Uranus people to learn to weigh the consequences of selfish and unilateral decisions against something that is more important, like reality, and relationships. The Spiritual Tests will be more on a material level of learning to live within their means and to practice self-denial for the greater good of someone else.

Minerva in the 2nd House of Values: Friends and family know they can trust these people and can confide in them because they sense inherently that everything that is confided is understood. If they only knew! Not only can Minervans understand them, they feel what they feel, see what they see, and experience both their pleasure and their pain. Minervan Beings, if they are balanced, also know what people are going to say before it is said, so there is no point whatsoever in attempting to lie to them. Don't think for a moment that they can be taken for granted or exploited in any way. They are street smart and experienced beyond imagination in the way of the world because they walk a much higher road than most, and they can walk in anyone's shoes.

Sun 2 in the 2nd House of Values: These people are not easy people to live with or understand. Wants, needs, and decisions in a partnership must be discussed and agreed upon in advance regarding almost everything. The ability to compromise is definitely a Spiritual Test in this aspect. If the partners will listen and state their own cases quietly, there is more harmony. Their Spiritual Test is to learn to value the opinions and feelings of others by practicing complete silence, and learn to listen without feeling the need to fix everything and everybody. Let the other person have their way sometimes. Sun 2 Beings must learn to pick battles that are important and not fight every battle.

Moon 2 in the 2nd House of Values: You are probably experiencing some fatigue because your higher self is going to "Love School." At this stage of spiritual transformation, it is expected by Spirit that you are also working universally on the physical plane in some direction to balance the energy equation of Loveforce energy, by writing, blogging, lecturing, teaching, and gathering positive and life affirming helpmates to do the work along the way. In this vein, it is important to remember that you cannot adopt or even help people into your life who are negative or energy draining, and not willing to do the necessary work to help themselves on the Earthly plane. Help those dependent upon you to break free of the need for your help.

Earth/Venus 2 in the 2nd House of Values: Earth/Venus 1 would have been concerned mainly for the comfort of their own families. Earth/Venus 2 Beings are much more active outside the home, and they have a larger family: a national, international, and universal one that they need to advocate for. Spiritual Tests in this arena call for proactive intervention to protect the innocent. All innocents. This Spiritual Test calls for stepping outside of comfort zones to face areas that require attention. It may not be easy for the loving Earth/Venus people as it may require more time away from home.

Mercury in the 2nd House of Values: This combination won't be what you might expect. Mercury people can attract money like a magnet, or they can use a magnet to find money. They are talented in finance matters. They will probably make more money taking the kind of chances that no sane person would ever attempt, and when they try to give money away, they'll make even more. As to families, they may have one, but not have a clue what to do with it except play with it and have adventures. The time they do give to their family has real substance to it. The time they give to *anything* has to have substance or they won't give it all.

3rd House of the Conscious Mind

Sun 1 in the 3rd House of Conscious Mind: We are energy beings given a body in order to enjoy the physicality of Earthly life. Nothing is as it seems on the one hand but on the other hand, Sun Beings in the House of Conscious Mind have a unique perspective on loneliness, and they understand both male and female energies within themselves and in their partners. They will advocate for equality on every front, and will be the most understanding parents in the world. Their capacity for love and caring and nurturing knows no boundaries.

Moon 1 in the 3rd House of Conscious Mind: Female energies are behind everything here. A male with this placement will have an innate understanding of women and his fashion sense should be relied upon. These people will have to guard against molding themselves to their partners' personalities to the point that they lose their own. It is a Spiritual Transformational Test in this placement: Moon Beings must learn not to change who they are for anybody. If evolved, Moon Beings will deal with this as they deal with everything else: bring it out into the light and address the issue right there.

Earth/Venus 1 in the 3rd House of Conscious Mind: Earth/Venus 1 Beings are grounded in the reality of loving, caring relationships, and it is unlikely that they will stay with anyone who doesn't reciprocate that love or that they will allow any kind of abuse. They will insist on being themselves and immediately try to improve everyone else around them. They will always champion the ones they love. The children of these people will know, beyond the shadow of a doubt, that they are loved. They are shown love in every way, and family life will be comfortable and generally happy.

Mars in the 3rd House of Conscious Mind: Mars, male or female, always has difficulty understanding the feminine, except in this aspect. They will be a natural negotiator and will try to solve problems with discussion and mediation rather than allow needless harm, chaos, or discord. They have a gift for smoothing ruffled feathers because they are empathetic. Mars Beings can be strong and forceful, never doubt it; and they may hide their more caring side, but it is there. If you have drawn this card two things can be going on: either you are trying to understand a strong individual who is giving mixed signals or you are this individual and are giving mixed signals. In any event, you aren't showing your true self and it may be time to allow some of the sappier thoughts and spontaneous actions to surface. Male or female, we cannot be whole without embracing both feminine and masculine energies. A Spiritual Test in this aspect is to be who and what you are without hiding anything you think people will reject. Balancing the male and female can be subtle and it can be done in the privacy of your home. If you are in public, be yourself, and don't be afraid that your fellows will mock you. You are a born negotiator and mediator, and really, your friends don't care. They are secretly wishing they understood people as well as you do.

Neptune in the 3rd House of Conscious Mind: Everything is perceived from the viewpoint of a loving outlook, so the natural home of Venus and Earth fall in naturally with this placement. Neptunians in this aspect may have difficulty distinguishing reality from fantasy. They may have visions, psychic inclinations, or dreams that are prophetic in nature. Many times those visions deal with the love aspect being abused or in need of healing. Neptunes in this placement must also watch out for self-pitying or destructive behaviors, which may come when they try to mentally process too much. Because of the ultimate femininity of this sign, a male with this aspect should be able to communicate beautifully with females and will be accepted widely in feminine circles. However, relating to the male machismo personality of others may be difficult for him. A female with this placement will have a small trusted group of female friends. When these people look at the physical and emotional side of life from afar, they may see this loving tendency as a weakness, but it is not. Loveforce is strong and can melt the hardest heart if the heart is capable of understanding true love.

Saturn in the 3rd House of the Conscious Mind: These people are really hard for others to understand. Their thought processes are very illusive and complex. Saturn people not only think outside the box, but their boxes are multi-dimensional. They are no-nonsense, street smart people, who only look gentle. Both males and females will have the look and behaviors of cats, and will tend to have bodies like gymnasts rather than muscle builders. They have everyone's number, and a firm grasp on the true reality of a situation. Because of this sixth sense, they have to be very careful about what they say: best to lead the clueless from layer to layer until they get a clue too. These Saturnians will make them think it was all their own idea in the first place, and even let them take credit for it!

Uranus in the 3rd House of Conscious Mind: Uranus people would do much better if they could learn to get out of their own way. Uranus Beings could choose to show the other side of themselves: the side that is strong and reliable in a crisis, and the side that can see problems coming, and foresee the solutions to forestall them. Uranus people are powerful, dynamic, and larger than life. They are, in truth, more Elementally balanced than most signs. They just need to play to their strengths, and quit letting the poor expectations of people they may have disappointed in the past keep them from seeking higher ground. The Transformational Test here is to break the pattern of life lessons getting harder and harder by learning from past mistakes, and accepting responsibility for them. Consider taking on a bigger projects for humanity, and giving without any expectations of getting back, or any thought of being admired for giving. Onward and upward should be the new battle cry!

Minerva in the 3rd House of Conscious Mind: The face these Minervans show to others is that of an understanding, patient, and competent mediator for everybody else's dysfunctions. People tell Minervans everything, and because Minervans are good listeners, and honestly do not appear to outwardly judge; they are often abused listeners. The people who control this abuse are obviously the Minervans themselves, but they've experienced enough of life in the shoes of the distracted and dysfunctional that they are almost immune to being shocked or dismayed over average people's capacity to misunderstand, misinterpret, and miscommunicate almost everything. The test of this placement is to rein in the tendency to try to save people. After a period of rest, you can come back renewed, but if the same scenario threatens to play itself out again with the clueless, withdraw and do let it be known, that the advice you gave them before hasn't changed, and you trust that they will work it out. Quit spinning your wheels with the lost and hopeless.

Sun 2 in the 3rd House of the Conscious Mind: Because this aspect is so complicated, life is always complicated for the individuals with this aspect. These people have a unique perspective on understanding that what we see is not all that there is. There is a measure of perception that extends to accepting the actual materialization of Spirit versus what appears to be seen. They understand bone deep isolation. Like Sun 1 in the 3rd House, not only do they understand the duality of our forms, that we are both male and female energies, but they understand an androgynous quality as well within themselves and in their partners. Their capacity for love, and caring, and nurturing knows no boundaries, and makes no judgement on what is 'acceptable."

Moon 2 in the 3rd House of the Conscious Mind: Moon 2 people are under the influence primarily of Venus, the quintessential mature love. The Higher Self of these people have earned a place beside Diana to help souls move from incarnation to incarnation and figure out their Lifescript plans for the next life. A Venuvian's concept of love is pure and envisions what mankind can aspire to, but never fully reach. They have no self-concept, no giant egos, or problems with esteem. They are selfless beings. They are complete within themselves, and if you are fortunate enough to have drawn this aspect, it is a spiritual message that you are on the right track to losing ego, and becoming a complete, mature spiritual being.

Earth/Venus 2 in the 3rd House of the Conscious Mind: Any man married to a woman in this placement knows "mom is boss" and accepts his fate. Conversely, the same would be true of a man in this placement. He will be a loving, somewhat strict father who is the head of the house. They are grounded in the reality of loving, caring relationships, and it is unlikely they will stay with someone who is abusive or doesn't reciprocate that love. They will insist on being themselves and immediately try to improve everyone else around them. The Spiritual Test, however, will be to let go, to relinquish control in an environment of trust and love. These beings must learn the lessons of waiting to be asked before giving an opinion or proposing a solution.

Mercury in the 3rd House of Conscious Mind: Mercury Beings have few illusions about being easy to live with. They know that like the metal for which they are named, they tend to melt under the slightest heat and flow away. It is a wonder to them, really, that anyone would be willing to put up with them. When they love someone enough to realize that their mercurial ways hurt them and the "running away" will no longer cut it, they can be dedicated partners in the relationship. In order for a mercurial love to be steadfast, the love interest has to be ready to flow too, and the lifelong dance that ensues will be non-traditional, magical, fun, and vibrant.

4th House of the Subconscious Mind

Sun 1 in the 4th House of Subconscious Mind: The Sun Beings here have an inexplicable need to run the other way once they have earned the love of another, even if the Sun Beings were the ones who pursued that love to begin with. They tend to sabotage relationships on purpose. They will almost always put their own need for personal freedom above another's need for reciprocal love. The Spiritual Test for this aspect is for Sun Beings to take time to be alone, and celibate, for a good long time until they understand why they never seem to get what they need. Then ask this question, "Do I give my partner what they need?"

Moon 1 in the 4th House of Subconscious Mind: The hidden part of us has very few acceptable outlets to release the pent up anger and frustration we feel. So what do we do? We handle the little things as they come up to try to keep them from escalating into big things. We have to learn to stop saying, "I'm okay, I'm okay, I'm okay" when we really are not. Dreamstate lessons from Spirit will emphasize respecting ourselves, and asking for what we need and want when we need it. That's a big deal with some of us. We give, but we don't take back. The deeper lesson here is to learn reciprocity.

Earth/Venus 1 in the 4th House of Subconscious Mind: Love is kind; but to not keeping some things hidden would be unkind. Brutal honesty is just that...brutal, and it is unnecessary. The Spiritual Test for these Beings is to think of the consequences of truth for others before indulging in the basic selfish need to have everything on the table, regardless of whom it hurts. These beings need to care so much about others that the pain of holding that tripping tongue is their pain, to be carried within, and not borne by others because of a need to speak. One can be truthful without causing pain. Diplomacy is the lesson here.

Mars in the 4th House of Subconscious Mind: People with this placement will always be a champion for the underdog. They will be a champion even when that underdog won't fight for themselves, nor does that underdog necessarily want a champion. These Mars Beings have had many lifetimes of fighting battles for people who have appreciated a warriors' help. The true test for people with this placement is not to help unless asked.

Neptune in the 4th House of Subconscious: This placement is quite unique and wonderful for Neptune Beings. Both Neptune aspects and the underlying energy of Mars balance each other out perfectly. Neptune People get to find peace and acceptance, and they are open enough to learn from night school lessons. This injects a new vitality and energy into the equation that generates more confidence. What is unseen is a natural tendency to aspire to greatness that is always held back by basic insecurity; but not here. This is a big deal because it means that the insecurities of Neptune and the aggression of Mars synergize into something else altogether: passion, vigor, energy, and a drive to accomplish. These people will be so charismatic they can accomplish just about anything they set their mind to. If they take on a project, it will be done and done well. Spirit's test in this endeavor is to teach Neptunians what it feels like to be balanced so that in future transformational movements, they can draw on their experience of one perfect lifetime in which they were "shiny."

Saturn in the 4th House of the Subconscious Mind: These people will be always be battling their emotional and psychological "demons" and must constantly guard against negativity ruling their lives. They must teach themselves not to react until they can process. This complex person understands subtle layers and connections and can see through deception and lies. They understand the criminal mind. The ability to understand dark thoughts and actions is a gift that can be turned to good. They might be the perfect person to understand, find or fight the bad guys, or heal the bad guys because nobody will spot darkness as well as they do in this placement The ability to recognize and fight gross imbalance or turn it around and heal it is their Spiritual Test. The ability to actually fight the darkness and corruption and destroy it is a *Fleur d'leis cleansing process.

*Fleur d'leis. The book, Spirit Speaks-The Transformation Connection by the author of The New Spirit Astrology System, Johan Adkins, goes *into protection and negative elimination methods, and it would be advisable for people with this placement to read that book.*

Uranus in the 4th House of the Subconscious Mind: These beings have sides to their personalities that belong to only them, and In all probability, nobody will ever know them fully. This placement can bring loneliness and isolation. It is the placement of karmic lessons: to tell meticulously the truth or withhold the truth if it causes undue pain, and to refrain from embellishing or dramatizing a situation. Uranus people are always a little leery of strong emotions and anger issues. Keep in mind that if small situations are addressed as they happen, they won't become larger issues that can backfire if handled in an aggressive manner. It is their test in this lifetime to find balance in the happy medium. One thing that will always help is gardening or doing yard work, and digging in or lying on the Earth to help get things in perspective. Ask for continued guidance from Mother Earth and the love aspect of Venus, and then be receptive to their wise counsel.

Minerva in the 4th House of Subconscious Mind: Minerva sits naturally in the 4th House of the Subconscious Mind, but Mars is the underlying energy, and with Mars comes issues of aggression and gross reality. Minerva lives in a rather unreal world of dreams, astral travel, and sleeping long hours to go to night school, but now those hours have a disquieting aspect. They may see things they don't want to see, and dream things of a prophetic nature that are disturbing. Because their energy is mutable to the situation at hand, Minervan Beings will be called on by Spirit to intervene in other dimensions and time lines. Their dreams will be realities to whole groups of people, and Minervans may be called upon to protect people from harm. Instead of just nudging those dream people or beings on the right subtle path to good decisions, they may actually have to nudge them to keep them from being harmed or killed. This aspect is a very difficult path for the Minervans because they are warriors at heart too, and have seen their share of gross reality; they just don't like it much, and would rather not deal with it in their dreams. The Spiritual Test here is to not turn away and shut this aspect out. It won't happen all the time, but when it does, it is happening to you because Spirit can count on you to help, so please help.

Sun 2 in the 4th House of the Subconscious Mind: Sun 2 energies in this placement have warrior Mars as the underlying Planetary influence. In order for the male dominated influences of Sun 2 and Mars to be balanced, Moon and Venus energy intervene, and make these people go to night school to balance the Loveforce energy that is unbalanced from this equation and combination. They must be sure to get at least ten hours rest at night, and grab quick naps during the day if they can. Even closing their eyes for ten minutes, and practicing deep breathing will help to calm troubled and turbulent seas. The Spiritual Test for this problem is to sleep, and go to school. Dream work and dream teaching is vital to the success of balancing Loveforce energy so these people may move on in the transformational journeys ahead.

Moon 2 in the 4th House of the Subconscious Mind: Moon 2 is advanced training. It goes beyond learning to deal with frustration and anger to enabling the Moon 2 people to do something about what is causing that anger. Think of this placement as being mother tigers protecting their kits. Anybody daring to get between them will be dinner. We can't literally tear someone apart for abusing our children, or any innocents, but we can certainly stand up for them, believe in them, and help them learn to address any wrongs being done to them. Not all of us are mothers or fathers, but we being asked to help guide innocents away from abuse, to protect them, and to help them to defend themselves, with a little help from their friends if necessary.

Earth/Venus 2 in the 4th House of the Subconscious Mind: These Earth and Venus Beings aren't very comfortable with hiding anything. Because Earth and Venus are primarily Loveforce energies, and one test of love is truthfulness and disclosure, hiding things in Loveforce is not second nature, but it is a necessary Lifeforce lesson for all of mankind. Love is kind, but to not keep some things hidden would not be kind. Brutal honesty is just that...brutal, and it is unnecessary. Truth can sometimes be held in reserve until the time is right to speak it. You can be truthful without causing pain. Diplomacy is the lesson here.

Mercury in the 4th House of the Subconscious Mind: Mercury Beings have always had a sneaking suspicion that life would not be this hard if only they could get away from it all for awhile. The only problem is, the reason they want to get away is to keep from having to deal with responsibilities. It's not exactly their fault; they have responsibilities galore in the Soulforce Pool. Behind all the flakiness of their freedom loving, Earthly lives, however, there is a deep-seated responsibility to everything and everybody. They will rise to the cause of the right and just, and they will take care of their families, but anybody who is close to them can tell you that loving these Mercurial Beings is like being married to Peter Pan.

5th House of Love Aspect

Sun 1 in the 5th House of Love Aspect: When Sun Beings love, they love with all of their soul but there is always a separate part of themselves held in reserve for their individuality that speaks every bit as loudly. A certain amount of freedom is needed by Sun 1 Beings, but too much slack in the leash will allow them room to roam. Unless they are with a partner that keeps life fresh and new and is interesting, diverse and valued, they may stray. If they are committed to the relationship, these charming stars have the capability to love fully and stay home. Just break out the costumes.

Moon 1 in the 5th House of Love Aspect: Neptune energy sits behind this aspect and tilts the love aspect to that of self-love. Moon Beings do not outgrow the need to feel acceptance from their parental units, or older people or mentors who stand in place of parental units. The Spiritual Test is for Moon Beings to take a step back, and rethink this whole need for constant reaffirmation of love. Try to see the loving things people do, and learn to recognize the unspoken support and daily care that that express love too. It is extremely hard to step out of the self and "let go and trust Spirit," but that is exactly what must happen to transcend beyond this aspect.

Earth/Venus 1 in the 5th House of Love Aspect: Earth/Venus Beings are traditionally motherly, natural, and comfortable in their skin. Venus contributes mature love and a willingness to fight and sacrifice for innocents. The underlying influence of Neptune adds the illusive and mysterious love that puts the self first. A man in this placement will have an innate understanding of women and the feminine, and a gift for sexual pleasure. This is a natural, happy, loving mix of energies, and the Sun-Creator energy can always step in with Lifeforce energy if the shopping gets out of hand. The true test of this placement is to extend the overabundance of love to the Universe.

Mars in the 5th House of the Love Aspect: Warriors can love their country and their fellow military brothers or sisters and possibly a mate, but the hardest test is to believe that they themselves are worthy of love. They must learn to love themselves first, and then that love can extend to others. Because of a fierce individualistic lifestyle and mentality, Mars lovers may be very difficult to love. They may place barriers in the way of finding love and once it is found, they will feel a need to see if it can be destroyed by tests at ridiculous levels. Loving Mars Beings is never easy, but it is worth the effort if you can resist killing them.

Neptune in the 5th House of Love Aspect: These people, although basically lovable, will have a very hard time believing that someone can actually love them. . Even if they open themselves sufficiently to accept that another mate "might" really love them, they will push the partner's love as far as they can to see if it can be broken. The Spiritual Test for this aspect, however, is to deserve the love that they test so indiscriminately and learn to respect that playing games with basic trust and their loved ones' tender hearts may backfire, alienating those they do love.

Saturn in the 5th House of Love Aspect: Saturn People seem like the perfect mates, charming and life loving as they can be, but there is always another side to the love equation with them: they are extremely intuitive, if not downright psychic, so there will be no opportunity for potential mates to deceive them. On the other hand, they themselves can be the masters of deception, the caped crusaders attracting potential lovers or mates like flies. Saturnians are looking for someone who can touch their souls. Saturn people live their lives a slight step off the planet. By that token, they may seem a little spacey and distracted, when in all probability they are sifting through a lot of potential realities to check where they are landing. If their reality for love includes you, you are lucky indeed. Peter Pan has landed on you!

Uranus in the 5th House of Love Aspect: Love is never easy. It is especially hard for people who see themselves as loving and giving but seem to be susceptible to others' using that love to manipulate and hurt. Love then becomes something else. It becomes not-love. The lesson for this placement: dump anyone who would abuse love this way. Don't waste love on those who are unable to love. Don't waste love on someone who would use and abuse you in the name of love. Spirit's test for you here is to love yourself enough to reject unloving ways. If you are already in a situation, make the decision to stay or go a totally selfish one. Don't consider the abuser's needs; just seek your own peace and happiness.

Minerva in the 5th House of Personal Love Aspect: People with this placement are looking for more than love; they are looking for a spiritual existence. They may find this love in a larger than life person who is of like mind, but they should wait to commit until they can truly call someone "soul mate." It is very important for these people not to jump into a long-term relationship with someone who can't understand the spiritual aspects of this kind of love. In any event, in order to be at a place where you can recognize your soul mate, some Spiritual, Emotional, and Physical housecleaning must be done with yourself first. Mates have to be capable of much more than being a good friend or just good in bed. They have to touch the soul.

Sun 2 in the 5th House of Love Aspect: Sun 2 is Creator energy, and understanding the female, and understanding love has always been the bane of his existence. Throughout all of time the Creator, as Zeus, as Wellspring Father, and as any number of hundreds of other names and personas he has worn, has enjoyed the companionship of female mates, but he says he doesn't fully understand females, and probably never will. They are an absolute enigma to him. If you've landed under this aspect, and are male, you definitely experience this same dilemma. If you are a female, you are probably even identifying with this as well. Females in this aspect don't fully understand their sisters either. With Neptune's energy adding an element of playful sexuality and possible kinkiness to this whole equation, it will be a challenge to deal with the basic matter at hand. The Spiritual Test that Wellspring Father keeps having to learn, he says, is to make every effort to get in touch with your feminine side; try to understand the females around you; study them as if they were anthropological test subjects if you have to, and see if you can get a better handle on it than he has. He loves females, and relies on them in every way; he just thinks they are having one over on him half the time.

Moon 2 in the 5th House of Love Aspect: Venus is the power sitting behind Moon 2, and Venus has rather an alien view of things. Their approach to problems and their reaction to the emotional involvement of mates and children is very often a step off from what their families and friends are expecting and needing. Venus Beings are fully transcended, and they are the masters of "wait and see" and "don't worry, it will all work out in the end." The majority of the time it will, but that doesn't comfort or resolve teenage angst. Moon Beings can be pretty strict but they aren't always understanding; this occurs not because they don't want to understand but because they are genuinely clueless as to what the fuss is all about. The Spiritual Test for this aspect is to really try to look beyond the immediately obvious with a different perspective. Whether or not the Moon 2 Being completely understands, sometimes all it takes is reassurance, a big hug and being the people who listen and care. Tea and sympathy and cookies or pizza can't hurt.

Earth/Venus 2 in the 5th House of Love Aspect: Sometimes we have to make hard choices. We have to give up something we want for something someone else wants or needs. The people who are under this aspect know that already, and they have already sacrificed a great deal for their families, their fellows, for the Universe, and for the Spiritual Pool. Sometimes the Universe recognizes a job well done and just allows some freedom to sigh and enjoy the experience of living in a solid body in an Earthly plane. Physicality is a gift, enjoying life in general and family life in particular may be experiences some spiritual beings have never had. Having tensile touch, and just being able to relish the joy of eating and making joyful noises; laughing with their children, playing with the dog and having family dinners with their loved ones, is something treasured by Spirit. This is one of those incidences, because if anyone ever deserved to just enjoy love and life, these people have certainly earned the right to "just be." If you have drawn this card, know that you are loved and appreciated, and Spirit wants the very best for you for a job well done. Blessings to you.

Mercury in the 5th House of Love Aspect: Mercury Beings are social and busy in general and will have a need to travel and have quality time alone. The partners of Mercury Beings will need to understand that a certain amount of freedom and distance from responsibility is necessary for their mates' happiness. Mercury Beings will always provide well for their families, and will love to cook but won't clean up the mess. If Mercury Beings don't marry, they will probably travel. They will have a huge bank of friends who are like family and they will never settle down for long with any of them.

6th House of Physical Aspect

Sun 1 in the 6th House of Physical Aspect: These beautiful people will be blessed with good self-esteem and innate understanding of the blessedness of all things. People with this placement will love to be outdoors, perhaps gardening, or being close to nature. They will understand the subtle changes in the Earth and heavens. They often have everyone confiding everything to them, seeking their advice.
These people are capable of sunny, positive, and life-affirming advice. They strive to help make others feel good about themselves and their decisions.

Moon 1 in the 6th House of Physical Aspect: Moon Beings like to mother everything, but with the charismatic and psychic Saturn energy underlying this placement, the possibility of anyone using this to manipulate them comes to a dead stop. No lie, no deception, no subterfuge will escape the perception of these Moon Beings. They will likely be made of sterner stuff, and will have the confidence to stand up diplomatically for themselves and anyone else being trod upon. These Moon Beings will be powerhouses of organization, mediation, and fundraising and masters at holding everything together. The Spiritual Test for this placement is to enjoy learning Lifeforce lessons and to be pro-active in their strengths.

Earth/Venus 1 in the 6th House of Physical Aspect: Saturn energy adds a bit of naughty and nice to an otherwise serious demeanor. Earth and Venus have always enjoyed attention, but in this aspect they have the added confidence from Saturn to act on some of their dreams. One thing is true almost without exception: these beings can sing like heavenly Angels, and whether they do it in the bathroom or in a concert hall, music will be very important to them. The Transformational Test for this aspect is to extend a helping hand to those who may not have the confidence in their abilities or dreams. Help someone else shine.

Mars in the 6th House of Physical Aspect: Combine the physical aspects of two dynamic energies of Mars with Saturn as the underlying background energy influence here, and you get psychic, beautiful, and dynamic. The challenges these beings face involve keeping their tempers and their mood swings under control, and ultimately, over the years, they will learn to do so. The Spiritual Tests for these Mars Beings are to learn to stay grounded, listen, and try to learn to empathize with others. It's important to allow others to talk, even though they might already know everything that person wants to say.

Neptune in the 6th House of the Physical Aspect: Because Saturn is the planet whose underlying power affects this placement, these Neptunians are more outgoing and confident than other people. There are energies at play that give them the confidence necessary to get exactly what they want and need. If you find yourself in this placement, you will be that person with just a little more chutzpah: the one people notice and listen to. They will want to help you because you're going to make it seem like the great idea you're talking about was theirs all along! So put on that cape of invincibility and go for it!

Saturn in the 6th House of Physical Aspect: These Saturnians are perfect chameleons and make excellent super spies. They love exposing different layers of the variety of personalities that make them so expertly adaptable As they get older, their self-perception may not match their outward appearance at all.. They remain forever young and forever playful and changeable.

Uranus in the 6th House of Physical Aspect: Uranus gets a break here. Saturn is the underlying energy, and it adds playful, fun, and intuitive life to what is usually a very heavy normal existence for Uranus. Uranus Beings finally have great possibility for healthy and happy relationships and their marriages will run much smoother. It takes awhile, however, in each lifetime for Uranus to make themselves stop and smell the roses without feeling the need to re-design the flowerbed into three acres of a labyrinth. Once they figure out how to make themselves relax and step away from obsessively working 24/7, they'll be much happier. The Spiritual Test is to stop and smell those roses and pick them for someone who needs a "pick me up." Get out of yourself occasionally and support the ones around you who have supported you so often. Take them some roses!

Minerva in the 6th House of Physical Aspect: Earth is the place of physical, emotional and spiritual trial and in this aspect you have reached the Earthly incarnation that will test your spiritual mettle. To move forward to Nirvana states or wisdom states, this life "upheaval" is a necessary process. The test of success and Earthly successful transformational state is the opening of the Hocaieah, the twin healing chakras located just under the collarbone. This is the time of life that we need to do a spiritual, emotional, and physical "housecleaning." Throw off the judgments of others and embrace the acceptance of alternative paths. Accept a new look, new ideas, and new philosophies. Sift through all the baggage and literally jettison what doesn't fit. Simplify, unify, purify, and balance. Dance, sing, and be happy. This process isn't comfortable. It often involves dredging up your personal "demons" and finally deal with them. People in transformational states must forego the judgment of others. Part of foregoing judgment is not accepting blame for the circumstances in the Life Path of other adults. Minerva Beings must learn to release control to be free.

Sun 2 in the 6th House of Physical Aspect: These people never seem to age. They maintain a youthful appearance and mentality their whole lives, and with the masculine energies of Sun 2 and Saturn combined, they exude sexuality, this allows them to attract whatever and whomever they want. There will be enough psychic and intuitive ability from the underlying energy of Saturn to know just what to say, when to say it, and to whom. If Sun Beings believe this to be true, they are deceiving themselves. What may be closer to the truth is that without some constraint, these people can be domineering and pushy. Other people will be lucky if they have a chance to express a differing opinion without being run over. The best part of this combination is that these Sun Beings are so attractive and charming that most people probably won't mind being trampled. Spirit minds, however, and the lesson here is to practice SILENT observation, and NOT to manipulate people or situations when it is so easy to do so. These Sun folks must learn discernment.

Moon 2 in the 6th House of Physical Aspect: Our powerhouse Moon 2 aspect just got barraged with extreme ends of planetary influences: Saturn and Venus, Loveforce, and Lifeforce in spades. They will be impossible to fool or lie to, and they aren't going to be the type of individuals who lie to themselves. They see themselves as strong, confident, and street smart because of Saturn's influence, and they like the fact that they are unreadable. They show you what they want to, and no more. It gets a little confusing because they will read everyone else, ferreting out every secret, and every confession, and people won't even know what hit them. One thing Spirit needs Moon 2 people to work on is tuning in to the quiet heart: the ones who don't pour out their souls; the ones who are quietly desperate, and need help but won't impose on others to get it. Just because people are silent doesn't mean they aren't in need. Find those people, and be there for them.

Earth/Venus 2 in the 6th House of Physical Aspect: The people who fall under this aspect have no clue how wonderful they are. They are some of the few of us who have lost Earthly ego: they have trusted their higher-powers, guides, or Spirit and "let go, and let God." They can take pleasure in the pleasure of someone else, and feel great joy for the accomplishments of another. As to how they perceive themselves, they don't care. They are neither traditionally male nor female. They don't fit into nice categories of body types or current trendy dress styles. They have a style all their own, and a charm all their own. It doesn't really matter to them if they wear jeans to a dress ball. Their confidence and splendor shines through from the core of their being, and reflects in the understanding in their eyes, and their countenance of being. If they do go to that ball in jeans, one look into their eyes will guarantee that the person dancing with them won't care what they are wearing either.

Mercury in the 6th House of Physical Aspect: Mercury Beings have pretty big egos, but to call them conceited and arrogant isn't really fair to the Mercury Beings. They are naturally skilled, lucky in business, and have a sixth sense for what will be successful and profitable and what won't. They are exuberant, enthusiastic, and gung-ho to bring great ideas to fruition, but they can't be counted on if things start to go south, and that is their karmic struggle. Mercury Beings will work hard on something they believe in with people who will work as hard as they. However, drop the ball and they will too; they'll move on to something else.

7th House of Emotional Aspect

Sun 1 in the 7th House of Emotional Aspect: The underlying energy of Uranus influences the Sun 1 Beings to make promises they can't possibly keep so that their loved ones are either continuously disappointed, or find it hard to believe in or count on anything they do or say. Sun 1 energy here tests these people to "make no promises, break no promises" in this aspect, and when they learn to stop promising things that can't be delivered, they will break a pattern of many lifetimes, and people will start trusting them again. The Spiritual Test will be to recognize that although they may want to please, they cannot please everybody. What they can do is try to please their Spiritual Guide and in doing so, life will be sunnier and happier.

Moon 1 in the 7th House of Emotional Aspect: The energy of Uranus underlies this aspect and Uranus presents challenges. With this aspect, finances may get out of control. Moon 1 Beings always center their lives on family, and because this is so, they strive for peace and comfort, but there may be discord instead. A Spiritual Test in this aspect is to learn the harder lessons from Lifeforce, which will only intensify and get worse if they are not addressed. It is also not a time to spend frivolously, relax the rules, forego restrictions, or tolerate errant behavior in children, especially teens or pre-teens. Be extra vigilant, but don't assume that the problem is what appears to be evident. *Listen to all sides* and be prepared to be a strong supportive parent.

Earth/Venus 1 in the 7th House of Emotional Aspect: Earth and Venus energies are in perfect balance and surprisingly so are the Uranus energies which sit behind the 7th House of Emotional Aspect. These people finally grow up to recognize that the needs of loved ones take priority over the selfish need to repeat the pattern of testing and retesting for acceptance. The Earth/Venus people grow to understand that the secret to happiness is loving something or someone else more than themselves. However, in order for this all to work, they have to learn to love the faces in the mirror first.

Mars in the 7th House of Emotional Aspect: When people are angry, they can't think straight. Sometimes situations that could be handled reasonably escalate into an argument or fight that blows the initial problem way out of proportion, with disastrous results. The real dilemma lies in whatever is behind the anger. Often it isn't anger over any particular incident, but anger over something unspoken or misunderstood. The male aspects of Mars and Uranus both sit behind this aspect, and neither is particularly warm and fuzzy when it comes to emotions. The key is to do the opposite of what you would normally do.

Neptune in the 7th House of Emotional Aspect: Neptune aspects represent sexuality, promiscuity, and destructive behavior in whatever House they show up in. Here it is in the House of Emotion.

Even more potentially problematic is the fact that Neptune is weighed too heavily with Loveforce energy and is inherently imbalanced to Lifeforce energy. This adds a tendency for narcissism into the mix. Take heart. There is a way out of the trap of alienated friends and family, loves lost, and one night stands. The Transformational Test of this aspect is to give of yourself in service to another. Make someone else happy.

Saturn in the 7th House of the Emotional Aspect: Generally, Saturn people have a lot of self-confidence, but here they face the possibility of obstacles placed in the way by Uranus' heavy energies. They should expect to experience not only a heightened level of perception, but also some elevation of fears and trepidations. Dreams may be more intense than usual. Psychic abilities will be tested. A cleansing and balancing visualization to help keep clarity and light in your world can remove any negativity. Faery sight is at the edge of your awareness and all you have to do is balance, cleanse, and open the third eye to see.

Uranus in the 7th House of Emotional Aspect: Emotions here can change from ecstatic to gloomy in the blink of an eye. These folks process everything, worry about everything, and face a hard life lesson if they can't learn to go with the flow more. The Spiritual Test here is for them to take a deep breath, just stop processing, and practice counting their blessings. They just need to enjoy the moment and try to live more fully, letting the little things go. Uranus in this aspect basically wants to be happy and wants others to be happy too. Everyone can be!

Minerva in the 7th House of Emotional Aspect: Minerva is the Dreamweaver, and she sits here in a house that is ruled by Uranus. Emotions run strong in mutable directions; therefore, an Element Card should be pulled here to understand the direction this aspect will take you at this time. This is the only aspect that requires readers to fill in some of their own gaps with an outside source. Minerva's energy is unlike any in the Universe. It is mutable, meaning that it molds itself against the need of a flowing river to help adjust the ebb and flow of the balance of Lifeforce and Loveforce, so it is always changing just as emotions change.

If you have drawn this card in response to a question and intend to just read one aspect, then here is the situation: emotions are out of control and you need to take some time to determine how to rein them in. If you aren't getting any rest and you are processing too much, Spirit suggests that you ground and center and choose an Element Card to help you determine which element you lack that will help settle you or the situation down.

If you have drawn this card in a full reading or comprehensive reading, then here is the situation: there is a teacher available to help you with the emotions surrounding your situation right now, and that teacher is the Element Card you will draw right now. It is possible that you have too much of the Element you will draw and it is possible you have too little, but the guidance you need to handle what you are dealing with is within the Element you pull.

Sun 2 in the 7th House of Emotional Aspects: People who have drawn this combination are struggling to understand the emotional picture of their day-to-day situations and their relationships in general. It is as if everyone else is an alien and has a view askew from the reality that people with this aspect share. It is probable that misunderstandings will ensue due to a lack of empathy to emotional turmoil, but these are the same people who can provide a cool head and straight thinking in a crisis, so hopefully the family and friends will be forgiving.

Moon 2 in the 7th House of Emotional Aspect: Women have always known that the cycles of the Moon affect mood and sometimes directly affect their menstrual cycles. The fact that women living together in close proximity will naturally coordinate their menstrual cycles should give us some indication of what is at work here. We are 90% water. We are interconnected water bodies, and the Moon's energy ebbs and flows within us, just as it does the tides. Expect some amplification here in the normal waxing and waning of emotions due to powerhouse energies converging (Sun 2, Moon 2, and Uranus) and try not to let the emotions overwhelm you. Imagine yourself immersed in a nice warm bath, and just enjoy and experience the excess. Don't always try to release emotions: learn to explore them, and allow them to be.

Earth/Venus 2 in the 7th House of Emotional Aspects: If Earth and Venus 2 are predominant, they will be so proactive in their advocacy for the underdog that they will be entirely consumed with resolving the issue. If the underlying Uranus energy predominates,

Uranus will not only expose the villains publically, and possibly legally, but this being will be adamant about making said villains pay, hopefully without smashing faces, and property damage. Uranus can influence others to be proactive as well, and, it is that side that will surface here and triumph in the end.

Mercury in the 7th House of Emotional Aspect: Life with a Mercurian is a series of comings and goings, and confusion. The people around these people are confused too. They pick up on the Mercury Beings' conflicting need to go, and their need to stay, and often get hurt because Mercurians will choose to go more often than stay. The "Oh, stick around, don't go" plea will send them running for sure. They can't mind you. They can't be held in check with demands or ultimatums. Think of these Mercurians like cats. Turn your back and appear disinterested in what they do, while keeping yourself busy doing something interesting or mysterious or mischievous, and they'll serpentine through the room just to watch you. They will want to stick around, and play too.

8th House of Generation

Sun 1 in the 8th House of Generation: Minerva is the energy underlying this placement and because she is moving, mutable change, this restlessness extends to the Sun 1 Beings. Having to be the "responsible one" is oppressive to them. They may deliberately sabotage their own success or advancement in a job if it is too demanding or oppressive. Sometimes, the family will just have to understand that these individuals have to get completely away from everyday everything and everybody for a few days. They will also have to clean their Spiritual, Emotional, and Physical houses in this lifetime, and that will require parting with negative, clinging friends and relatives, eliminating as many material goods as possible, and addressing that need for private physical space and understanding.

Moon 1 in the 8th House of Generation: Minerva is the energy behind this placement in the 8th House of "What is," and while this may not be what we want it to be, it truly is where we are on our transformational path. If Moon 1 Beings are balanced Elementally, they are right where they should be. Although we are primarily two main Elements, we experience living in and receiving teachings from all of the Elements throughout the course of our spiritual lives.

Transitioning from one to another isn't always easy. We cannot be "fully cooked" until we have experienced them all. Spirit's test in this aspect is to learn to "go with the flow" of the current Elemental teacher, and to try to relax and learn from the Element.

Earth/Venus 1 in the 8th House of Generation: Earth Element people are grounded, rooted, and like to be close to the Earth. Their deep connection to the Earth is something that the other signs crave and rarely feel. They are tied to Mother Earth and their mothers will be important. These Earth/Venus 1 beings tend to observe the situation and process before they decide what is going on. They form their own opinions. Earth Element people are loving individuals, and are loved by their families. The Earthly Spiritual Test is to stand up for the underdog and not condone abuse. Their Venus lesson is to love and teach others to love responsibly.

Mars in the 8th House of Generation: Mars People are take charge, move into action kind of people. Since they first go to the physical as a way of handling things, Minervan teaching sets them asks a pretty hard task: it asks that they think first and observe, not react; and that they watch the natural progression of the consequences of how things flow. If you've drawn this card, Spirit is asking you to be patient, be observant and try to let those around you make their own mistakes. The Spiritual Lesson is also to teach others not to always rely upon you but to rely upon themselves. Success will suit them and make them proud of themselves.

Neptune in the 8th House of Generation: Neptune's water affiliation causes people with this aspect to ebb and flow in their decision-making, and the heavy Loveforce power structure confuses the issue further. They are constantly searching for an avenue to give the overwhelming love they feel to one person but they consistently fail to find the one true love to give it to. The Spiritual Test for this being is a tough one. They will have to start off being alone and then learn to give some of their unbounded love to themselves before extending it to anybody else.

Saturn in the 8th House of Generation: Saturn Beings have a multi-dimensional skew on everything. They think quickly and so far outside the box that it is scary. Minerva sits as the mutable power behind this aspect, shifting the energy wherever it needs to go for the good of the Saturn Beings, and the work they are trying to do for Spirit. Minerva's purview is dreamstate teaching and astral travel.

Saturn Beings will be going to night school, and using their additional gifts of psychic perception and dimensional thinking to deal with universal problems. This is an exciting and dynamic opportunity to create a fine balance in life and for Saturn Beings to gain the confidence that they can do anything!

Uranus in the 8th House of Generation: Minerva, the underlying energy behind this sign, puts a heavy load of dream teaching, dream weaving, dream walking, and astral projection in the night life of Uranus Beings. Your pre-conceived view of reality is seeming hazy, disconnected and wacky. You're just not getting enough rest. A few naps and early bed nights should set you right. If Spirit or your family is making too many demands, talk (meditate, pray) to their higher selves and ask them to tell the physical bodies that you need them to back off to let you rest and regroup.

Minerva in the 8th House of Generation: Minervan Beings are always operating with one step off the planet and moving toward their personal transformational path and toward oneness with Spirit. Because of direct spiritual contact with the Creator, Minervans are also receiving a constant stream of "data" that makes dream states and fantasy very real for them on many levels. If they will use the gifts given and own them, they will live a more normal life. The Spiritual Test for these beings is to understand that they are blessed of Spirit and as such are expected to help when they are asked; and they will be asked.

Sun 2 in the 8th House of Generation: The Sun Beings in the 8th House of Generation are struggling with issues of faith. They are struggling with the day to day, and feeling out of step with it. They are also struggling with having to be the responsible people upon whom everyone depends because it is oppressive. Minerva influences this placement and Minerva has itchy feet. At the same time that Sun people try to be good employers, employees, husbands, wives, or parents, they are wanting and needing to run away from it all, and may sabotage their own success or advancement in a job if it is too demanding or oppressive. They are not necessarily irresponsible or uncaring, but they can be. On a deep inherent level they feel that they must have a great deal of alone time in order to regroup and recoup their busy minds. The Sun Beings may have a completely different set of friends with whom they enjoy a certain amount of freedom. These individuals are often spacey and distracted and have a tendency to day dream. They have a lot of unanswered questions that only they can answer. In this lifetime they are tasked with cleaning their spiritual, emotional, and physical houses, and this requires parting with negative, clinging friends and relatives, and eliminating as many material goods (except toys) as possible.

Moon 2 in the 8th House of Generation: After this many incarnations in their Earthly physical life, these Moon 2 beings are becoming warmer individuals, more in tune with the emotions and needs of others. The biggest change in their higher-self work, is their ability to more fully explore the richness of their dream lives. They've learned to slip in and out of other dimensions either in sleep phase or astral projection. They've also honed their skills of empathy and sympathy and are learning to not only "walk" in the shoes of another, but to psychically sense in projection where pain and suffering enter and what to do to help. This is a very exciting and vital association because Minerva can transmute whatever energy these individuals need when they need it, exponentially increasing the ability for the Earthly individual to help heal anything. Spirits' test for this placement is to put those skills to work to help others heal themselves and help Spirit heal everything. Be on the lookout for entities who are in trouble.

Earth/ Venus 2 in the 8th House of Generation: The Venus lesson for these beings is to love and teach others to love responsibly. They tend to have strong family values, and strong attachments to an extended family. They are tied to Mother Earth and their mothers will be important. The Spiritual Test of an Earth/Venus 2 in the House of Generation is to not only stand up for the underdog, but to also advocate, and protect them at possible personal risk.

Mercury in the 8th House of Generation: Mercury Beings are just cute. They are funny, generous, attractive, vital, and a royal pain. They're slippery and hard to hold onto. They like to travel, and they love to interact with everything and everybody, and typically, they don't have to work too hard to have everything come to them. However, this can cause problems, because while they will attract people who burn with desire for them and want to be with them. Mercury Beings are generally clueless about the effect they have on others. If you are the person attracted to Mercury Beings, enjoy the individuals you are attracted to as really good and true friends, however, unless you are both single, don't risk a stable, loving relationships to be together. The Mercury Beings won't stick around, and it is very unlikely they will give up their families for you. Be kind to each other, and don't let it go there.

9th House of Regeneration

Sun 1 in the 9th House of Regeneration: People with this placement are being given Spiritual protection and guidance throughout their lives and are being trained to join Spirit in the Soulforce Pool. They are doing Spirit's work on Earth and may have to accept that others may not understand this. The Sun is the revitalizing force for this individual and will channel the necessary energy and instruction to do what is asked. Prepare to listen.

Moon 1 in the 9th House of Regeneration: In this lifetime, the Moon Beings need to accept that they are doing Spirit's work on Earth, whether or not others may understand. These people will be working with others to teach the love aspect, heal the Loveforce balance, and promote love in all things. Their highest teaching is living love, the most shining example of these people living their faith without the need to be recognized or rewarded for it. They will understand true humility, and indeed may be Angels returned to Earth after having transcended, on some task from Spirit. They will feel white light spiritual presence, and hear the voice of Spirit provided they stay balanced male to female and elementally. The Sun is the revitalizing force for these individuals and the Sun will channel the necessary energy and instruction to Moon Beings in order that they may do what is asked.

Earth/Venus 1 in the 9th House of Regeneration: Because this individual is blessed with the possibility of perfect balance of Lifeforce and Loveforce energy as well as a blessed life, an Earth/Venus 2 placement is expected to give back. Spirit will test this individual by asking for help and healing. If the individual stays balanced, they can hear cries for help from the Godhead and/or Soulforce Pool, and they must be prepared to help. They must answer the literal spiritual phone or doorbell when it rings at all hours of the night or day and listen for instructions. Say," I hear you, what can I do for YOU?" three times and then be amazed when they answer.

Mars in the 9th House of Regeneration: If Mars Beings have reached this point, they are well on their way to finding love, peace, and happiness on the Earthly plane and deep spiritual fulfillment when they incarnate again. For now, Mars Beings can just enjoy being happy. They are finally ready to start looking for partners, and if they've found their soulmates, Mars can finally relax and enjoy that miracle.

Neptune in the 9th House of Regeneration: Here, Neptune People finally have a chance to shine in the positive aspects of their traits. They will be working with Spirit now in a very real way to heal the waters of the Earth and to address the issues of pollution and protection of the planet's struggling Water creatures. These beings help to balance the Elemental aspect of Water with the other Elements. They will be working with higher souls to teach them about the Water Element, and will be helping others to acclimate to Water. That is the Spiritual Test of this aspect; selfless devotion to the success of another.

Saturn in the 9th House of Regeneration: More than any of the other planetary signs, Saturn people can hear Spirit all the time and that gets a bit overwhelming. They get so inured to the constant psychic chatter that they can't or won't pick out the important from the unimportant chatter which clearly becomes a problem for them. What has to happen in order for Saturnians to proceed down the transformational path is for them to ask for a threefold blessing of a quiet mind with a designated guide and it will be a godsend for this aspect. "There can be only one."

Uranus in the 9th House of Regeneration: Uranus Beings, like determined and faithful drill sergeants, choose to put themselves and others through the paces. The reward for success, however, is great. There is a hierarchy in Spirit, and one of the most sought after placements in the Soulforce Pool is that of the Creator's trusted inner guard: the Walkers. Among other duties, Walkers are the Spirit Guides of soldiers and protectors. Uranus Beings will be Metal affiliated, and that's a big deal. The Spiritual Test for the 9th House is for Uranus Beings to stay balanced male to female, and start working in their higher selves in dreamstate in night school with the Metal Elementals and Vortex.

Minerva in the 9th House of Regeneration: The people with this aspect will be able to direct their dreams and work inter-dimensionally and extra-dimensionally to help other Beings choose the right path in their spiritual journeys. If you've drawn this card, this may be what is happening: you are having dreams that seem so real that the people in them feel real too, as if they are precious long-time friends or family. You've stumbled onto one of your multi-dimensional lives. Ask for direction from your Divinity Cards and before sleeping, ask Spirit (three times) to help you understand what you need to do to help.

Sun 2 in the 9th House of Regeneration: These people are Angels on Earth and must act upon the direction given. In return, they get the gift of having physicality again and can enjoy sensory touch and smells, a good meal, a happy healthy home, and loved ones. They may also be expected to heal the sick or work with the energy matrix of the Universe to heal the Universe too. They can do the work quietly and alone with the help of a few like minded friends, even if the friends are rocks, animals, or planets. The Spiritual Test is to stay balanced, revitalize in the Sun, and listen for instructions from a quiet voice surrounded by white light.

Moon 2 in the 9th House of Regeneration: Diana, the Creator's mate, was given responsibility for the Moon and the Earth. She sees the souls first after death, and is responsible for helping them in rather a limbo stage between lives to determine where they will go next. If they have cleaned up their spiritual houses, they may be ready to join the Soulforce Pool, but if there are lessons they want to learn or if they desire another physical life, they must incarnate. Before they do, they task themselves with the lessons they must learn and others agree to help them by assuming roles in their lives as mothers, fathers, husbands, etc. In this House of Regeneration, and at this stage of transformational maturity, these people may be tasked by Spirit to return as Angels with a specific job to do. These people have the Creator's attention, and if they are very well balanced, they can talk to him. What they need to ask, however, might surprise them. They need to ask the Creator, "What can I do for you?"

Earth/Venus 2 in the 9th House of Regeneration: The House of Regeneration is a house of ascension, but in order for Earth/Venus 1 individuals to get there, they have to learn a great deal in this lifetime and be on this path for awhile. They have to be balanced Elementally and male to female; they have to have experienced the rise of kundalini; and they have to pass the tests of the Fleur d'leis.*(See footnote). People earning this status can join the Soulforce Pool after this incarnation. Needless to say, the tests are tough, but the attempt is well worth the journey. It is transcendence. If you are this Earth/Venus person, be prepared to work hard and know that you are blessed to be doing this work.

Mercury in the 9th House of Regeneration: These Mercurial people dream of travel, and the love of travel will be a lifelong love. They are blessed of Spirit, and if open, will receive direct spiritual contact and teachings. This contact may require that these people go here, do this, meet this person and possibly convey a message. Even if they are not open to being directed in their travels, they will nevertheless have the urge to move, and keep moving, constantly. They can expect at points in their lives to experience the visitation of walking Spirit. Be aware that the person in the right place at the right time lending help or asking for help, might be sent to test you or be there as a messenger or protector.

10th House of Universal Lifeforce

Sun 1 in the 10th House of Universal Lifeforce: This Sun 1 placement is such a balance of heavy-hitting feminine energy that it sets up a perfect yin and yang of the energy of Loveforce/Lifeforce. In the world of Spirit, there are those who are destined to be reincarnated lifetime after lifetime, not because they need to be, but because they want to help do Spirit's work on Earth as an Archangel. If you have this aspect in your Full Chart or Soul Chart, you are one of these beings. You are very aware of who you are. You hear Spirit clearly, and when well balanced, you have probably experienced seeing spiritual entities as well. It is a given that you have "faery sight." It is very likely that you will be called upon to do Spirit's work on Earth, working nightly in Dreamstate to help. This placement is blessed indeed, and the Transformational Test that you will have from Spirit is to play your blessings forward, to be both teacher and student.

Moon 1 in the 10th House of Universal Lifeforce: To be whole people, we have to have a creative side. Any creative endeavor that people have spent lifetimes perfecting is art. Creative endeavors serve spiritually to help balance the Universe. Sometimes the best help we can give Spirit is to finally work on the model airplane sitting in the closet, and daydream while we do it. What can be imagined can be created. What is envisioned as healed and whole, and beautiful can be made manifest. If this combination is drawn or if it is a part of the comprehensive reading, Spirit wants to applaud your artistic and imaginative endeavors, and ask that you continue creating, and maybe to sing while you do it. They love singing.

Earth/Venus 1 in the 10th House of Universal Lifeforce: Earth is the training ground for spiritual trial, and Venus is the aspect of the test of love in this lifetime. This is the perfect placement to study universal love and to learn to understand the spiritual connection. In order to be well balanced, the Earth/Venus Being will have to learn to operate with Lifeforce energy and practice saying "no" when instincts say to say no. A test may be tough love at work or at home, and the ability to love the self enough to stand up when it counts.

Mars in the 10th House of Universal Lifeforce: By the time Mars warriors reach this placement of Universal Lifeforce, they are expected to have battled their demons, forgiven themselves for being alive, and moved on towards working hard on that love thing. If they aren't there yet, they aren't listening to the Angels whispering in their ears constantly guiding them; *and they have great guides*, the Sun/Creator, and the Moon/Diana. Their higher souls fight a good fight all night long, and it isn't inconceivable that the fatigue felt is battle fatigue. People with this placement have set themselves the task in this lifetime to defend and protect in one dimension or another. That is what they are doing and what they must continue to do.

Neptune in the 10th House of Universal Lifeforce: Dolphins and whales sing healing to the Universe. From under the seas they sit in two dimensions and work tirelessly to heal Loveforce energy for planet Earth, for the spiritual realms, and for every transcended being on the planet Earth. As a Neptune Being, you will forever be tied to water bodies and the Water Element, for you sense your responsibility to keep things flowing. In this House of Universal Lifeforce, you must lose your ego. Spirit will place many opportunities in your path to practice "not calling attention to yourself." When you finally "get it," you'll be an Angel on Earth and you will be able to move on in your transformational path.

Saturn in the 10th House of Universal Lifeforce: When Saturn Beings reach this point, they have started to settle into comfortable dialogue with Spirit. They are actively working not only in dreamstate, but perhaps in waking dreams or visions during the day as well. If they have arrived at this juncture, they will be able to settle their lives down in general and start paying attention to what is important: their friends, their families, their chosen professions. This aspect will allow them to be less stressed, more caring and more attentive to their mates, living in the moment for once, without needing to talk, or to be doing other things at the same time. Saturnians get to just "be" in this placement.

Uranus in the 10th House of Universal Lifeforce: Life will get easier now because Uranus Beings have finally broken negative patterns that result in the Life Lessons being repeated. They are searching for the higher road and spiritual path. Spirit is whispering in their ears and for the first time, they can hear. Working for Uranus Beings is their inherent balance of male to female. Relationships will be working better in this lifetime than ever before, and difficulties can be handled. The spiritual search is ongoing, but now there is light at the end of the dark tunnel and these people are finally able to walk into the light.

Minerva in the 10th House of Universal Lifeforce: Spirit requires that the people in this aspect be balanced male to female. Minerva, being mutable can help there. Minervans also have the guidance of the trinity to help them accomplish Lifeforce training. This must be done in dreamtime, or in literally walking a mile in another's shoes. It requires that help be offered so that those needing guidance, advice, or help can learn to accept it gracefully. The Spiritual Test is to become selfless in this regard to help other entities attain their goals.

Sun 2 in the 10th House of Universal Lifeforce: Trust your instincts and gifts. You are in a singular position to offer healing to the Earth, the creatures of the Earth, the rocks and water systems of the Earth, and the energy of everything. You are blessed with the gift of healing, and moving energy on a cellular or a universal level will be easy for you. The trick is to keep clear, keep good things in your body, and don't pollute the vessel of Spirit's work...you. What is offered is earned increment for the cause of love and healing. What you visualize you can create. Instruction and guidance and messages will come in dreams or waking visions.

Moon 2 in the 10th House of Universal Lifeforce: They have to grow up spiritually and make themselves get off the fence to act if an innocent is threatened with harm. The other spiritual task for the higher-self of these beings is to do some soul searching for their next incarnation. They will sometimes feel like an alien in a touchy feely world that they no longer can identify with, and consequently, they may have some personal issues in relationships. Take heart. This is a tough lifetime, but eventually things will start falling into place and some peace can be reached. How? It's a miracle!

Earth/Venus 2 in the 10th House of Universal Lifeforce: Like Janus, it is no surprise that we also have two faces. We are all both male and female and in this House of Universal Lifeforce, we are being called to keep the balance equal between the two parts of ourselves. Those who dwell in this position are tasked with harder lessons of protecting and being proactive for the innocent. They must advocate for the underdog. They must love the unloved and defend the weak. Whether they are male or female, they evolve to become the ultimate mother and father.

Mercury in the 10th House of Universal Lifeforce: Mercury was a messenger of the Gods depicted as having wings on his feet. In their most secret hearts, people with this placement want wings too. They want to take a message and travel with it to the ends of the Earth. If they have something they want to say, then it must be said at some point in their lives, even if it has to be secretly. If these people do not literally travel to spread the message, they must branch out to friends and family and perhaps wider groups of people to share the message where they can. These people have the ability to influence others. They can sell what they promote and believe in. It is a natural gift.

11th House of Universal Loveforce

Sun 1 in the 11th House of Universal Loveforce: This is a big picture, and a big blessing. It is very possible that the Sun 1 Beings with this placement will spread the message of love and Spirit's teachings to great masses of people if they are so inclined. It is just as likely that they will live their life in quiet anonymity, simply enjoying the blessing of direct spiritual contact and universal teaching. On either path, they will be blessed with direct contact from a higher form or lots of higher forms, depending on their personal belief system. Either way, the blessing extends to giving these people peace. All they have to do is listen and live their lives in such a way as to be able to hear.

Moon 1 in the 11th House of Universal Loveforce: At this juncture, they are seeing that love must extend beyond to a much bigger Universal Loveforce picture. The ills of society, our culture, our families, and even many of the ills of our Earth can be healed with love. Moon 1 people have an abundance of knowledge and experience to light the way. They may find that they involve themselves in community service or counseling in some form. They are definitely in a position to mediate problems for other families and communities, to organize awareness programs, or just roll up their sleeves to help build a homeless shelter or man a food bank. They have already done a lot of the hard stuff to earn their transformational place. Remember, this aspect addresses not what one *intended* to do with their lives but what actually was accomplished. A Spiritual Test would be "When you are sitting at St. Peter's gate, and asking to be let in, what did you do to promote love in the Universe?"

Earth/Venus 1 in the 11th House of Universal Loveforce: No means no. This is pretty simple really, but it does take a great deal of courage to say no in the first place and even more when the no is dismissed as *maybe* or *later* or just ignored completely. This is not acceptable. Spirit expects these Earth/Venus people to stand up for themselves and for innocent others. When someone threatens your job or your body, it is time to fight back. Because this aspect is weighed so heavily in the feminine underlying energies of Earth, Moon, and Venus, it might seem fluffy, but it isn't. Those feminine aspects are powerful, proactive, and strong. Sun stands behind this aspect too, so a lot of guidance is provided in how to deal with disrespect. Respect extends to fighting for the planet, and in this position, it is expected that Earth/Venus people advocate for Mother Earth too.

Mars in the 11th House of Universal Loveforce: When warriors have to do battle, it wears on the heart, hardening it and making it difficult to love without also dealing with the possibility of loss. Major powers of Earth 2, Venus 2, and Moon 2 energies stand at warriors' shoulders. The feminine energies will help to soothe the pain and heal individuals; helping them to look at the world with more loving eyes. If those who draw this card don't see themselves as warriors, it is understandable, but in all transformational paths, we have all been warriors in many lifetimes. The other part of this placement is that these people will be called upon not only to love, but also to know when to use tough love. However, they need to be able to discern when to be tough, and when not to react and to trust their loved ones, and just listen.

Neptune in the 11th House of Universal Loveforce: Life will be much richer and fuller than you've ever experienced in any other lifetime. This lifetime will be a joy, likely spent in service to others. The satisfaction you'll experience enjoying their accomplishments will be monumental in your life and in theirs. Spirit is hopeful that you will be proactive for the creatures of the Sea and the health of Earth's waters. However, even if you are not actively advocating for the Water Element on the Planet, you are doing the work you need to do in your sleep. Enjoy this sweet life that you've worked so hard to earn!

Saturn in the 11th House of Universal Loveforce: Saturn people have always enjoyed psychic and intuitive skills, and by now, they have learned to fine-tune their talents. They've always had a view slightly askew, and when it was based around ego, it generally acted as a self-serving instrument. However, in this aspect, any negativity in this regard is transcended. Anything done in Universal Loveforce has to be done as both teacher and student and in loving sacrifice to the greater good. At the point where Saturn Beings deeply experience the joy of heartfelt wonder for the success of another, they are on the right path for losing the ego and for oneness in the Soulforce Pool.

Uranus in the 11th House of Universal Loveforce: You are reaching a maturity where the drama and the chaos that you normally project or get involved in should be minimal, and you won't need it or want it in the future. It is important to the future journey of your soul that you direct your energies now to a broader scope. It is inherent in this placement that you actively pursue your social, political, or intellectual interests that affect not only yourself, but your planet. You are expected here to broadcast and use that great power to raise national and international consciousness to help save humanity from itself and to protect Mother Earth.

Minerva in the 11th House of Universal Loveforce: Minerva is mutable energy, which molds itself to the individual needs of the astral traveler. Yes, it is dream teaching, but in this house, it is more dream molding: *creating* a reality for someone or something for the good of the Universe as a whole. Minerva is tasked to work with the Vortex who create our perception of physical life. If you've drawn this card, life just got a little more complicated. Your love has exponentially blossomed into understanding universal love, and loving things means protecting things. Minerva is well suited to teach you this. Much of the work will be done in your sleep, so be sure to go to bed early, and stay balanced in order to remember what you learn in night school.

Sun 2 in the 11th House of Universal Loveforce: This is a big picture aspect, and it is also a big blessing. People with this placement will be called to spread the message of love and Spirit's teachings to great groups of people. Alternately, they may choose to live their lives in quiet anonymity, doing their work quietly and simply, enjoying the blessing of direct spiritual contact and universal teaching. They are given an understanding of the lessons of universal love, joy, and peace. All they have to do to enjoy this blessing is to fully stay balanced in every way, listen, and live their lives in such a way that makes them able to hear.

Moon 2 in the 11th House of Universal Loveforce: People who have reached this point have buried their personal demons. They are influenced only by the need to help people understand that love must be the answer to the chaos of the world. They will all be spiritual leaders in one form or another, even if that means they will live their lives quietly and silently. They will be working with the Universe to spread the energy and concept of love and fighting darkness where they find it. They are powerful spiritual warriors. They are all, in one sense or another, Universal Prophets for love.

Earth/Venus 2 in the 11th House of Universal Loveforce: The people who draw these two cards are being tasked by Spirit to advocate for Mother Earth, and all the planets in all solar systems. The higher souls are helping other souls transition from their Earthly bodies to their spiritual bodies, helping them discern which Life Path lessons and challenges they must face if they must reincarnate. They work with the Fleur d'leis,* those entities chosen by Spirit to assist them in healing and teaching on Earth. They have what Spirit calls, "earned increment," which is spiritual blessing, protection, and guidance directly from the Creator.

Mercury in the 11th House of Universal Loveforce: Wellspring Father was weary of the responsibility of his creations but had to make sure they were cared for. Adonis had the responsibility of their care. Mercury is just one persona of a God created by the Sun, Wellspring Father. Adonis was Mercury's other name, and he had to be responsible for the Universe. That's a big job, especially when he had to balance, universally, the two energies of Loveforce and Lifeforce. So the solution was to merge the energies to balance Loveforce with Lifeforce and a universal dance ensued to mingle the energies. It really wasn't easy to do as the Planets were, at one time, divided Loveforce and Lifeforce. So all of life had to change and that change came about in 1994 with the Jupiter comet. Because, if the planets did not accept the basic energy change, life in the Universe would have ended instead of the comet breaking up on Jupiter. If it had hit in one place, it would have knocked Jupiter out of its orbit, and it would have knocked the other planets in our solar system out of kilter and that would have been the end of life on planet Earth. Luckily, they all got into line by accepting a change in their energies, except Jupiter.

For the people drawing this card, all of this explanation is necessary as background, because you are facing a spiritual test of Loveforce. An event, or series of events will happen that will make it necessary to stand up for someone else. You may not actually have to fight or kill, but you must not turn a deaf ear or a blind eye to either violence or mistreatment of a fellow being. It won't necessarily be another human being, it may be a mistreated animal. The other Spiritual Test here is to become more aware of the needs around you.

Watch the struggle around you and help.

12th House of Karma

Sun 1 in the 12th House of Karma: All souls returning to a new incarnation start here. Although it is the Twelfth House, it is actually the first house that individuals come to after deciding what they will be learning, teaching, and experiencing between one lifetime and another. Incarnations still earning Soulforce Pool transformation must ultimately balance male and female incarnations in order to fully incorporate the masculine and feminine energies in their being. On top of this, there is the matter of dealing with a new Elemental teacher. All souls have a primary Lifescript Elemental guide, but if they are having difficulty, it may be because the souls aren't used to their Elemental in this incarnation. We must ultimately deal with all six Elements in their time in the span of our lives. This is what it means to be balanced Elementally. One clue as to what Element is currently prominent is one's "favorite" color. Look in your closet and see if there isn't a color clue!

Moon 1 in the 12th House of Karma: Mercury is an underlying energy and influence on this placement. Mercury is travel, adventure, and on the negative side, escapism, whether that escape from reality involves drugs, alcohol, or negative adventures on the Earthier side of sexuality. With this placement, there will be immediate karma for things done against the higher good of the individuals or their friends or family. If people with this placement will seek spiritual guidance from the feminine side of themselves or their friends or family, they can follow the natural side of Mercury, just having adventures in whatever they do. Instant karma works both ways here. It can bring great blessings for great good.

Earth/Venus 1 in the 12th House of Karma: Earth/Venus Beings begin their journey in a house where they can't get away with anything. There is instant karma for any wrongdoing against anything of a pure heart, and to boot, there is a kicker. The harm, negativity, or bad vibes wished upon another return three-fold upon the ill wisher. That's a lot of broken mirrors. The saving grace is that there is also instant three-fold blessings for good work and good thoughts. It is so very unlikely that these people will be anything but loving and giving, and wonderful.

Mars in the 12th House of Karma: Mars Beings have earned their place in the Soulforce Pool if this aspect shows up, and it has taken many battle weary lifetimes to get here. Mars people get to just enjoy life for once with very little or no responsibility to Spirit in their higher lives because they have passed all of the tests with flying colors. The House of Karma always carries a three-fold blessing for great good, and conversely, three-fold problems if pure heart beings are harmed by people of this aspect. The odds of that happening are very low because Mars Beings have learned to love; themselves and others. If they slide into old patterns once in awhile, Spirit will forgive that too, because Mars Beings have "earned increment" from Spirit. Mars Beings are blessed by Spirit, and under Spirit's protection, as are their families.

Neptune in the 12th House of Karma: For Neptune Beings to reach the House of Karma, they have had to learn many lessons. The biggest one was to learn to love themselves unconditionally before they could love another. They have learned to lose the egos that chained them to behaviors that only made them and those around them unhappy. That is no small task, but they have passed these tests. They have learned to help with all aspects of the Water Elements, and are working to both heal the planet, and help their fellow Water Beings. They have even passed the tests of the Elementals. They have had to deal with being all six Elements by now, and that makes them much better rounded. As with all signs in the House of Karma, they can relax and enjoy their Earthly lives, living under the three-fold blessing of instant karma. They are so amazed and thrilled to be in this aspect in their higher selves, it is very unlikely they will have to face the three-fold retribution part of harming a pure heart. On the Earthly side of this, these Water babies will have a hard time not being on the beach or immersed in water to dance their joy! Of all the signs that may travel to follow the Sun, it is likely that many of them have this aspect in their charts. Spirit wants them to enjoy their accomplishments and blesses, and thanks them.

Saturn in the 12th House of Karma: Bravo! For Saturn Beings to reach the House of Karma, they had much to overcome. They had to fine-tune their psychic and intuitive skills to a master level. They had to calm all the voices in their heads and ask for and receive one guide, one voice. In doing so, they have found a peace and happiness they have been searching for for a multitude of lifetimes. This sign is the mark of a truly evolved soul who has worked hard to get here. They will still have to pass the tests of three-fold blessing and retribution and meet Spirit's Life Script, but as a reward for "earned increment", Spirit asks only for occasional help so that Saturns can enjoy their Earthly lives, their friends and families and a peace they have never known before.

Uranus in the 12th House of Karma: Bravo! Uranus needs to be congratulated, because it was extremely difficult for them to get to this point. Because this is the House of Karma, the Life Script will be determined by Spirit, and the three-fold blessing and retribution will apply to this incarnation. Spirit trusts that Uranus Beings have finally have matured enough to succeed. In past incarnations, these beings have been sorely tested, but they determined the Life Script themselves, now Spirit designs the Life Script. Now they are expected to have learned the three cosmic laws of responsibility: we own our own souls; we are responsible for our own souls; and we alone must take the consequences for our decisions and actions. Spirit is betting on their success!

Minerva in the 12th House of Karma: You have a lot of work to do in this lifetime to assure that your soul will continue on in the transformational journeys ahead. You need to pass three tests: Physical, Emotional, and Spiritual to achieve Fleur d'leis* status for your soul to live past this lifetime. You may feel the need to have a spiritual journey, egged on by the many nights of dream teaching, or spiritual instruction during the day that lead you to DO SOMETHING. Spirit will never ask you to do something wrong. It may be as simple as stopping your car to give that street person $10.00, but you'd better listen, and not be afraid to act. That street person may be God in human form.

"Fleur d'leis" is a not a misspelling. It is really it is an older spelling which means, "Flower of Lifeforce" in the stone or Pen'l Leina-Language. The Fleur d'leis process for Physical, Emotional and Spiritual housecleaning is explained in the book, Spirit Speaks-The Transformation Connection by Johan Adkins.

Sun 2 the 12th House of Karma: Those who love the Sun 2 individuals will have to understand their need for a Spirit Quest. If their family is lucky, they will come back, but they won't be the same. Traveling and having time to reflect will answer some questions, but more questions will likely come up that require more time for answers. If it's any consolation, the Sun 2 Beings' quest has nothing to do with their jobs, friends, or family. It does not mean love is lost, or that the Sun 2 Beings are looking for something or someone else. They are, in fact, looking for themselves. .

Moon 2 in the 12th House of Karma: Mercury is an underlying energy in the House of Karma. With Moon's water influence here, and the fact that Mercury is liquid metal, this escape from reality might easily become a flow into problems with drugs, alcohol, or negative adventures into the Earthier side of sexuality or life. The House of Karma is the final testing ground. Seek spiritual guidance from the feminine side of themselves or their friends or family to stay on track. The upside is that Moon's influence of Loveforce/Lifeforce energies can overcome Mercury's allure and karma works both ways. It can also bring about great blessings for great good. Love conquers all; it can conquer this too.

Earth/Venus 2 in the 12th House of Karma: People with this aspect have to fight the fight for Earth, for the survival of the human race, and for the survival of the creatures of inner Earth as well as for those upon her surface and in her skies. What can be imagined can be made manifest. They must also shoulder the task of protecting Mother Earth in her transformation as well. What is dreamed can become reality, so dreams will eventually take on visionary qualities, as these beings are also tasked with possibly traveling the Earth (physically and astrally) to spread the message to love. Their message is simple: stop hurting the Mother.

Mercury in the 12th House of Karma: Mercury people are preparing to join the Soulforce Pool and stop the incarnations. They will have the ultimate journey home. Mercury has been a messenger, and people often want to kill the messenger. Spirit has been telling them to "endeavor to persevere" because the Earth is dependent upon its messengers for continued survival. Friends and family of Mercury people at this juncture will either understand that Mercury has a higher duty, or Mercury people will do what they need to do without their support. The charming Mercurial children have grown up and they have important work to do.

GLOSSARY AND SOMETHING ELSE.
Aspect
Meaning of a sign or composite meaning of two signs.
Aura
Energy levels surrounding an individual like layers in an onion, which have swirling colors and chakra systems in all layers. The aura is how Spirit sees us. They don't see our physical body, just the pattern that our auras define as us. Our auras meld into the auras of everyone. We are interconnected and are truly parts of the whole. One person can affect a whole room, or even a whole community if they are imbalanced and their aura is "muddied."
Balance
Equal energy between male and female aspects of each of us equal energy between the six Elements and equal energy between the physical, emotional and Spiritual sides to ourselves. When the energies are equal, we are in balanced, when they are unequal, we are imbalanced.
Cleanse
Bathe, clear, clean and put in order your body, the sacred space, and your home. Metaphysically, a cleanse is more: it is a return to purity from a position of possible impurity or corruption. If the decks are left out of their natural order and sprawled across the coffee table with cigarettes and beer, there is no way you will get an accurate reading from them. They have to be cleansed of the negativity first by ordering them in their natural order and honoring them with a cleansing of white light visualization, and a cleansing of elements to restore them to purity. If you want to be privileged enough to speak with Spirit directly, respect their communication devices.
Elemental Energy
In The New Spirit Astrology System there are six Elements: Fire Element, Air Element, Water Element, Earth Element, Wood Element, and Metal Element. Traditional astrology

deals with four Elements and Eastern astrology adds Wood Element and Metal Element.

Emphasis Cards

Emphasis Cards help to pinpoint the main points of the reading to narrow down the options available for interpretation. The readings are always all three: Physical, Emotional and Spiritual, however one or two may be primarily where Spirit would like to see you concentrate on. *Spirit Speaks-the Transformation Connection* by Johan Adkins goes into hand charts which supplement this teaching.

Fleur d'leis

People think this is a misspelling, when really it is an older spelling of the term, which means, "Flower of Lifeforce" in the stone or Pen'l Leina-Language. What this involves is a deep look at and cleansing of any residual hatreds or a sense of things left undone, in order to forgive, forget, or let go of and move on. These beings will have physical, emotional, and Spiritual Tests to pass. The book, *Spirit Speaks-the Transformation Connection,* channeled in part to Johan Adkins, gives very specific instructions on how to find out where you are on this journey. The Fleur d'leis teaching is also available there.

When people achieve this status, a lot changes. They feel an increased awareness; they can move energy in any direction; they have the ability to hear and see Spirit; and they have increased ability to work with the Elements, Vortex, and the creatures of Earth, sea, and sky and deal with negative energy and transmute or destroy it if necessary. Their skill at creative visualization is extremely powerful, and they can literally create what they imagine for the Universe. This requires mature and forward-thinking analysis of the situation. Their abilities to heal all things will increase, and they will have an innate understanding of what to do. They will really earn their spiritual symbol of the fleur d'lys. This traditional French symbol represents many things, but historically it is a symbol of protection and honor. The Earth/Venus 1 people earning this status can join the Soulforce Pool after this incarnation. Needless to say, the tests are tough, but the attempt is well worth the journey. It is transcendence. If you are this Earth/Venus person, be prepared to work hard and know that you are blessed to be doing this work.

House

In The New Spirit Astrology System, the Houses number 1-12, but they are not traditional astrology Houses. Even if the names are similar, the values may differ substantially. The Houses help tell us the general area in our lives that we are working on; the basis, the values of money and finance, home values, attitude toward family, love aspect, how we view ourselves, what emotions are at play, etc.

Imbalance

Imbalance is a term of Spirit denoting the opposite of balance. Many people want to see a more acceptable spelling of "unbalanced" but imbalance is something else, it is a term referring specifically to the opposite of; equal energy between male and female aspects of each of us, equal energy between the six Elements and equal energy between the emphasis areas of Physical, Emotional and Spiritual. When the energies are equal, we are balanced, when they are unequal, we are, according to Spirits vernacular, imbalanced.

Lifeforce Energy

There are two energies that intertwine in the Universe in a dance of yin and yang: Lifeforce energy, which can be understood as "head oriented"; and Loveforce energy, which can be understood as "heart oriented". They interplay between the Planets and Elements and Houses in The New Spirit Astrology System and the ultimate power structure determines the aspects.

Life Path

This is often referred to as Life Path Script because it is the plan written by our higher selves in-between lifetimes for the lessons we will learn in the upcoming incarnation. The Life Path Script details are never known in the new incarnation but when the lessons we set for ourselves are not learned, we get to repeat them over and over and they get harder each time until we finally learn them. If the lessons planned for this incarnation are not learned, then the soul has to re-evaluate and decide how to address that. In the final count, we have to be balanced male to female lives, so perhaps our souls will decide to have the same lessons as the opposite sex, for example.

Loveforce Energy

There are two energies that intertwine in the Universe in a dance of yin and yang: Lifeforce energy, which can be understood as "head oriented"; and Loveforce energy, which can be understood as "heart oriented". They interplay between the Planets and Elements and Houses in The New Spirit Astrology System and the ultimate power structure determines the aspects.

Pen'l Leina

Stone symbol language, means "Pen Line." See *Spirit Speaks the Transformation Connection* by Johan Adkins for details.

Planet

In The New Spirit Astrology System, the Planets that affect life on planet Earth are in a delicate balance and exchange of Lifeforce/Loveforce energy between themselves and the Sun. Just a few of the Planets affect mankind's transformation and some, like Jupiter and Pluto do not enter into the equation at all, because they don't exchange the energy necessary to have any effect.

Spirit...and something else: Johan Adkins' Story.

In order to define Spirit, I guess I finally need to tell my story. When I first started channeling, I was an agnostic. I couldn't accept or say that I was talking to God as I was being told I was. I'd had an imaginary friend as a child, who I'm now sure was an Angelic guide. I had also heard voices trying to speak to me, which I blocked out for years, thinking that I was crazy or schizophrenic or something. At one point when I was twenty or so, I was just doodling when suddenly my hand took off and started automatically writing. That experience scared me, but it also fascinated me. I started learning everything I could about metaphysics, shamanistic practices, healing techniques, stone healing, handwriting, automatic writing, calligraphy, channeling, astrology, numerology, light work, divinatory systems, and so on. I searched for years for my own spiritual puzzle pieces, and I thought I had my puzzle fairly done.

In 1994, I was without a job. I was walking down 18th Street in Cheyenne, Wyoming. I passed an empty storefront and noticed the phone number. I called it and arranged to rent the space. I never even processed what I was doing until it was done. I called my husband and told him, "Well, I guess I have a job now. I just rented a storefront."

That storefront became the Prism Metaphysical Center. Helpers, partners, teachers, Shamans, and Medicine People came to help me, guide me, and teach me. I picked up the doodle pen again in the form of a pendulum and the pendulum started writing. Spirit taught me to hear by also allowing me to see what I was hearing through the pendulum. Eventually, I just sat at a typewriter and volumes and volumes of data streamed through my fingers, as if my fingers were "hearing." I didn't relinquish control of any part of my body except my fingers. As I was typing, I was reading what I was typing. It was like reading a novel written by someone else.

I only channeled when I felt love and light surrounding and protecting me from any negative influences. I was fairly steeped in Native American philosophy at the time, so I could accept that I was talking to a higher power, but I still couldn't rectify it in my mind that I was talking to God, nor did I necessarily believe in God. I told the voices so and they said, "We believe in you."

I channeled portions of two books between 1994-1995, *Spirit Speaks* and *The Transformation Connection* but because I didn't want one read without the other and was afraid of reactions to what I had written, I waited almost fourteen years to publish them. I only really had the courage to publish because my dad's sister, my soul Aunt, Norma Smith, read the manuscripts and admonished me. She told me, "This isn't yours to sit on. It was given to you in trust and you have to publish it for everyone." So I became my own publishing company, and when my English and Latin professor, Pat

Landy, agreed to become the Managing Editor for Bon Nuit Publishing (I deliberately named it *Bon Nuit* in improper French instead of *Bonne Nuit* just so I could use the subtitle, "Excuse our French"), we published my two visionary fiction books first, *Prismland* and *Earth 1* in October 2010. Just prior to the books launching, I gathered up my courage and quickly published *Spirit Speaks-the Transformation Connection* as one book. I published the book without it being edited as I so agreed with Spirit. As a publisher and writer, that makes me cringe, but I understood the messengers' reasoning. Too many times in history their words have been "edited" and the meaning and intent have gone straight out the window.

In 2008, during that time I was sitting on *Spirit Speaks -the Transformation Connection,* The New Spirit Astrology System was born. The sheer volume of the work overwhelmed me because Spirit wanted me to write it by giving me the just the basics and the general system. I worked on it sporadically for two years before throwing up my hands. It was shelved in partial completion for another few years. The messengers forced its resurrection a year ago by systematically nagging and making me dream about it night after night. I only agreed to finish it if they would help write it to assure the accuracy, and they had to let me edit it.

I was looking through some tarot sites and fell in love with Gloria Jean's Infinite Visions work. I contacted her and asked if she would agree to do the artwork on part of the astrology cards and to my delight she agreed. Spirit agreed she was perfect for the project, so I picked it up again and **voilà,** here it is.

Believe me, all of this is coming to a point.

As white light channeling has continued in me for over a period of twenty-five years, it is easier for me now to shift into the process. Over this time, I've had to extend my credulity to embrace the existence of the higher powers who spoke to me; to accept more than one God, and more than one Goddess. I've spoken to Planets, Directional Beings, Elements, Vortex, Rainbow Beings (inner Earth Beings), Stone People, Flower People, Medicine Wheel Council, creatures of the Fire, Earth, Water, Wood, Metal, and Air and sometimes alien beings; the Minervans and Neptunians and Jupiter Beings, who also work for the benefit of Earth. The fact is, they are all really part of one thing: members of the Soulforce Pool, which centralizes around the Creator energy of the Sun. The Creator, who has taken many forms and many names over time has currently adopted and loves being a Dragon and calls himself Sentinel. (I think it appeals to his sense of the macabre.) In any form He takes, He is the Creator, the "I am". Everything comes from Him and that which he and his mate Diana created. Adonis, (one of <u>his</u> many names) is his "split apart," the *better* part, He says; who is the other side of two-faced Janus, the being the Christians call God. The three of them created everything in the higher dimensions and the dimensional pool or Soulforce Pool of transformed souls who evolved into the Godhead. It's also called the Angelic Realm, Heaven. I call this (and they call this) <u>group mind of transformed souls</u>, **"Spirit."**

I am not an agnostic anymore, but I am certainly not a traditional Christian. I've just had too many experiences, too much proof, and documented miracles happen around me for me not to accept that for whatever reason I was chosen, I am being blessed with divine instruction, intervention, and healing energy.

Physical holy people and creatures have revealed themselves to me through the years. Spiritual contacts have amazed me, surprised me, and scared me; tested and retested my belief systems, and caused me to throw out everything I thought I knew and understood.

I have faery sight, so I see things most people miss. I believe we all see this realm; we just program our brains not to register it. My spiritual puzzle has taken on dimensional and interdimensional form. I realize now that time is not linear. You can also call me delusional if you want, but I have personally met God. He came to me in the form of a man about whom I've written about in my books *Prismland* and *Earth 1* (I named him Spero Zezas) and much of what I presented in those books as visionary fiction is actually true. He walked through the door of my metaphysical center,

Prism, in 1994 when I was particularly down and feeling misunderstood and rejected by the community. The love and energy that surrounded him was so intense, I grew to understand and know eventually who he really was. When he smiled at me, he immediately became my best friend. He was undeniably holy and his message was, "If they come up against you, Darling, just dance with them." The entire store vibrated and lit up with energy, love, and light every time he was within two blocks of the store. I always knew when he was coming to visit. He gave me the benefit of his friendship, teaching, and whimsy for too short a time and then one day, he was just gone.

He was named Adonis in another time, long, long, long ago...

Soulforce Pool

Heaven, The God-head, the oneness in which all souls eventually reside after earning their place by; living a balanced lives male and female, balancing all six Elementals and passing the Fleur d'leis Tests of transformation. Suggested reading, *Spirit Speaks-the Transformation Connection* by Johan Adkins.

Soulpath

The New Spirit Astrology System does not necessarily deal with birth charts, but it does deal with Soulpath Charts and readings. Soulpath is the journey our souls make through many lifetimes toward transcendence into the Soulforce Pool and the Godhead. For the purposes of simplification, Spirit has given us the New Spirit Astrology System to explain the steps that are necessary for transcendence. Our souls must move through hundreds if not thousands of lifetimes from chart to chart until we graduate through all twelve charts. At that point, we are Transcended Beings. The 12th House of Karma is the final test and in this House, we are given tasks to perform by Spirit, and our report card reflects in whether we have to incarnate again or if our souls may reside in the Soulforce Pool.

Three-fold Request

The New Spirit Astrology Card System is designed to give you the best chance of direct communication with Spirit. Spirit's attention is attracted by repetition, that is why different religions across time and space rely on mantras and repeated prayers and entreaties. When you wish to speak to Spirit or ask for assistance in a reading; the first request rings the doorbell, so to speak; at the second request they open the door; and the third request they are there with you, waiting to talk to you. If you feel strange stating your request three times, you can say, "I ask this the perfect way, the perfect number of times," and that also gets their attention. You risk not getting an accurate reading if you don't state your request in three-fold form.

Vortex

The Universe has the same structure as a cell, the surrounding cell wall is Metal Elemental matrix, and where two or more matrix strands meet, these points are called Chakras. Chakras are like tiny tornados in their energy structure and chakras are vortex and energy within the chakra is also called vortex. Vortex is not many beings, but one conglomerate, and so they are referred to not in the plural, but a singular group word, or simply as Vortex. Vortex has the job of keeping the chakras in the matrix healthy, but it also provides the illusion of reality, and continuity for the souls living physical lives. Confusing, I know, but if you think of atoms forming objects and grouping densely together, the structures they create appear to be solid, but nothing is truly solid. It gets even more confusing when you consider that the Vortex also separates our dimensional and interdimensional lives. We live many lives in one or separate dimensions on time lines that don't truly exist. Time is not linear. It is the responsibility of the Vortex to keep us from running into ourselves, and to sufficiently separate the realities to allow us to be unaware of simultaneous lives. If we get close to meeting ourselves, or even beings who are close to our other selves, we get very disoriented and confused; we rather unravel. Unlike basic science fiction accepted facts, we will not unravel time or cease to exist if we touch, but it is highly unlikely that we will ever get close enough to touch. We will suddenly feel a driving need to go in the other direction.

Closing Comments from Johan Adkins

We are Universal Beings who are intrinsically linked to one another, so much a part of each other that one person who is imbalanced can muddy everyone's auras and effectively imbalance a whole room. We've all felt the vibes. Somebody walks in and everything changes, conversation stops or lags, and people look over their shoulders.

I've taught hundreds of people to trust their instincts, the little voices they hear that guide and warn them. We are powerful beings in our small Universe; what we perceive can be created in not only our reality, but also in other dimensions. Negative thoughts, ill wishes toward another, constant bickering, talking and not listening, griping, complaining, blaming, expressing anger, fear and worry may indeed cause problems to those around us and especially to ourselves. If we perceive that there is "evil", we incorporate that perception into dark energy that muddies our auras and can gather with other dark energies to recreate that which we perceive. Yes, bad things have happened and some people are malevolent, I agree; but true "evil" is gone from our Universe unless we collectively create it again. People may be grossly and horribly imbalanced and may do terrible things, but in the eyes of Spirit, they are redeemable. We are all redeemable... and have our whole lifetime to make amends if we have wronged someone or something.

A mother's song to her baby will comfort and soothe, choirs will raise the vibration in a room so high that we feel the presence of light and love all around. Spirit's message in this book is clear. We can fix this. We can fix everything. We just have to work on balancing the Loveforce energy together and envision wholeness, healing, health, strength, love, joy, and brotherhood for all of our fellow beings as well as for ourselves.

Because we are loved.

ABOUT THE AUTHOR

Johan Adkins has been studying various branches of metaphysics and healing techniques for a lifetime. She owned and operated Prism, a metaphysical store for a number of years, and has taught hundreds of people metaphysical aspects.

She is a publisher with Bon Nuit Publishing and the author of a channeled work called, *Spirit Speaks-the Transformation Connection*, and two visionary fiction books, *Prismland*, and the sequel *Earth 1*.

She has been a healer all of her life and comes from a family with similar and extraordinary gifts. She now travels all over the world, writes and futzes, and works with Spirit doing what is necessary for the Universe.

She resides in the West in the boonies with a husband, and has two children and two grandchildren.

BOOKS BY JOHAN ADKINS

SPIRIT SPEAKS-THE TRANSFORMATION CONNECTION (ON KINDLE ALSO)

PRISMLAND (ON KINDLE ALSO)

EARTH 1 (ON KINDLE ALSO)

THE VERY LITTLE WHITE BOOK OF NEW SPIRIT ASTROLOGY

THE BIG WHITE BOOK OF NEW SPIRIT ASTROLOGY (DUE TO COME OUT ON KINDLE)

ORDER BOOKS THROUGH THE WEBSITE
HTTP://WWW.NEWSPIRITASTROLOGY.COM/INDEX.HTML

JOIN US ON FACEBOOK

JOHAN ADKINS, AUTHOR; BON NUIT PUBLISHING; NEW SPIRIT ASTROLOGY

PINTEREST AND GOODREADS, JOHAN ADKINS

WEB PAGES JOHAN ADKINS
HTTP://WWW.NEWSPIRITASTROLOGY.COM/INDEX.HTML

TWITTER; JOHAN ADKINS

LINKED IN; JOHAN ADKINS

SYNOPSIS OF *PRISMLAND* AND *EARTH 1*
BY JOHAN ADKINS

Prismland and Earth 1 are about families of young people dealing with arson and attempted murder, homosexuality, cutting, and the death of a loved one. But it's also about riding horses and working on a ranch in Wyoming, getting lost in a cave, dragons, fairies, alter universes, astral travel, Genghis Khan, and Quetzalcoatl. Now, if that sounds improbable, read the books and see if author Johan Adkins manages to pull it all off into anything remotely resembling a cohesive visionary fiction tale for young adults.

In the final analysis, it's mainly about a young girl, chosen by a record keeper crystal, to save Earth and her task of finding twelve people to help her save the Universe as well.

If you think no self-respecting author can possibly tie this together, then you can add to the mix Angels and mythological creatures like Zeus and Diana, Aphrodite and Aeneas or just ask Spero Zezas, possibly the most charming Walker Elf you'll ever love to explain it further.

BOOK REVIEWS

WRITER'S DIGEST MAGAZINE
PRISMLAND

Congratulations to Johan Adkins, Bon Nuit Publishing and Editor, Patricia Landy!

Writer's Digest has reviewed *Prismland* by Johan Adkins for the 17th Annual Self-Published Book Awards and rated an average of 4.5 out of 5 on plot, character development, grammar, and cover design and gave this positive review.

"What a good read. I enjoyed both your real world and your fantasy world. You did a good job of characterizations. You did a fantastic job of showing the relationship in both the Vanderlin/Selph family and Postelwaite families and how the past has impacted the family members. I liked how you showed there being another aspect of the bullies that while not excusing their behavior, at least explains a possible reason for it. I especially liked how you presented the beating

of Peter without the reader having to experience how bad it was, yet understanding how bad it was. The father made a great villain, and I liked that Spero gave Nels the chance to change so that when he caused the fire, the reader felt that Nels did it to himself. I was interested in your impression of Genghis Khan being like Robin Hood and linking him with the Rainbow World. Interested enough to look that up sometime. You did an exceptional job of explaining how the Rainbow World can be explained with a God that doesn't violate or contradict the religious beliefs of your readers."

WRITER'S DIGEST MAGAZINE
EARTH 1

Congratulations to Johan Adkins, Bon Nuit Publishing and Editor, Patricia Landy!

Writer's Digest Magazine has reviewed the sequel to *Prismland, Earth 1* by Johan Adkins for the 18th Annual Self-Published Book Awards.

On a scale of 1-5 (5 being excellent) They rated the Plot at 4, Grammar and Proofreading at 4.5, Character Development at 4.

Although *Earth 1* didn't win, I'm pleased with their evaluation and great comments.

EXCERPT FROM *EARTH 1*
Reprinted with permission of Bon Nuit Publishing and the author, Johan Adkins

Spero woke up early and disassembled from Bette's house and reassembled in Peter's room in the hospital. Peter was sleeping. Spero did a quick scan of the condition of his body and his injuries. He put his hand on Peter's head and sent healing energies to the puncture wound. He could tell it was deep and would result in infection. The doctors would take off the dressing this afternoon and pronounce him ready to go home, and his fever wouldn't climb, and the wound wouldn't become septic like it would have a few minutes ago.

Peter opened his eyes and saw Spero standing over him. He looked down at his leg and back up at Spero. "What did you do?"

"Just sent a little extra healing your way. What did *you* do?" Spero looked at him solemnly.

"Stupid stuff. Ma called you, huh?"

"Yes. She was pretty upset."

"Well, I didn't want to upset anyone, I just….I don't know… I felt like I was going to explode if I didn't do something."

Spero looked deeply into Peter's eyes and his look was sad. "I want you to promise me something, Peter. I don't want you to hurt my really great grandson ever again."

Peter said slowly, "Whaaattt??"

"My grandson, Peter. I don't want him hurt, even by himself. Would you like to hear a story?"

Bette had come to the hospital early too and was just outside the room. She had been there long enough to hear what Spero said. She leaned against the wall outside the room so that she didn't interrupt their conversation. She wanted to listen too, so she hugged a comfortable wall and stayed there.

"Once upon a time there was a lonely God. He had a lot of names, but one of them that the Greeks liked was Zeus. Zeus existed alone and got tired of talking to himself, so he visualized the most perfect mate and all of the attributes he could possibly wish for her. He wished and wished and 'whooosh' he extended enough of his lifeforce, elemental, visionary, and dream energy to

create a lovely mate. He named her Diana. The mythology books say 'Dione' but it was really Diana.

He and Diana loved each other so much and together created an expression of that pure love in the form of a baby daughter who was the most beautiful baby in the whole world and her name was Aphrodite. Aphrodite didn't grow up like most children; she was alone because Zeus and Diana were busy visualizing and creating other deities to rule various aspects of the world they envisioned. They wanted to populate and rule their new world, Olympus, which is now called Rainbow World. They had long discussions about ruling it wisely and together as regent and co-regent. Zeus visualized many creatures that you saw there and they have stayed the same through the years.

Aphrodite was always surrounded by multitudes of strange creatures who kept a watchful eye. The woodland creatures known as the Oreads or Nymphs, adored the child and cared for her every need.

She grew up wild and free but was kept separate from the other gods and goddesses. Because she was so beautiful, it was feared by Zeus and Diana that she would introduce an aspect of love that their creations had yet to experience and were not mature enough to deal with. She would teach them jealousy and cause strife because every man who looked into her eyes would fall in love with her and would do anything to have her.

So to keep this from happening in their new world and to allow her a normal childhood, Zeus and Diana sent her to Earth to live alone. She was not really alone; she was surrounded by and constantly doted upon by her beloved Nymphs, as well as by the Earth People, Tree People, Fire People – the Astanagas, Air Beings, Fairies, and all the sea creatures you met and more.

Aphrodite loved the sea best and she was always safe there, because everything in the sea loved her back.

She was natural and wore no clothes and the sun even seemed to kiss her skin, never burned or discolored it. She had long white-gold hair like your family and large blue eyes.

Now remember that the water element shares dimensional space on Earth and in Rainbow World. Sea creatures on Earth can exist simultaneously on Rainbow World.

Aphrodite was happy until she was fully grown and then she became aware that she was one of a kind on Earth. She had nobody who looked like her.

One time when she was riding her very young dolphin friend and swimming in the sea, they followed a beautiful mermaid to a sunken kingdom that Aphrodite had never seen before. It was named Atlantis. The mermaid entered an archway and there was a bright flash and she disappeared.

"Take me there, Bontitu."

"It is too deep, mistress," the Dolphin replied.

"Then go very fast!"

Bontitu was very young or he would have known he was not supposed to take her so deep and never was he supposed to take her to the portal, for it led to Olympus.

They both took great breaths and Aphrodite flattened herself against the dolphin's back so they could go even faster. The Dolphin rushed through the doorway and there was a 'flash' and they came out on the other side in a sea cave.

Aphrodite arose from the bottom of the sea in a great rush of water and foam on the back of her dolphin friend. The mermaid who had just come through was beside herself. She didn't know what to do because Zeus had entrusted all of her people to guard that Aphrodite never found her way to Olympus, and there she was. Aphrodite had to go back right away before someone saw her.

But, there was a catch. Now that Aphrodite was here, she could never go back. If beings came through in their heavy bodies, they split themselves into two entities who existed simultaneously in both places. They were aware of their split-apart self for the rest of eternity, existing in both places, but never again could they reunite. The portal that brought the beautiful Aphrodite here would not open again to take her back because now there were two Aphrodites.

The Aphrodite on Earth would age and eventually die and the Aphrodite on Olympus would stay young and live a long, long, life because, as you know, time passes differently there. The Aphrodite on Earth became known as Persephone. More about her later.

In that cave, a group of Olympian gods and goddesses were bathing and having a picnic. Among them was a god named Hephaestus, who was the god of Metal or they say of 'smithing.' He wore a beautiful golden torque that he had crafted himself. Contrary to myth, he was not ugly. He had bronzed skin and was tall and muscular and beautiful. Aphrodite was drawn to him instantly. Also, she had never seen anything crafted of such shiny metal glistening in the sun before. She seductively and unashamedly walked over to Hephaestus and touched the golden torque. She met his eyes and he was immediately in love.

The problem was, any man who looked into her eyes was also immediately in love and this was the problem Zeus and Diana hoped to avoid. The gods fought among themselves, and when Zeus became aware that Aphrodite had returned, he placed her in seclusion in a palace of women.

Remember I said that Aphrodite was natural? Well, she taught all of those women to enjoy their beauty and their bodies. and their sexuality. She was rather a bad influence, and as a result of that, was known as the goddess of sexuality and carnal love.

Hephaestus crafted beautiful jewelry for her and an intricate golden cestus, or girdle, that caused even more stir among the males of Olympus. Zeus decided to marry her quickly to Hephaestus, and they were sent to live in seclusion. They eventually had a son, Aeneas.

Aphrodite was restless and she missed the women's court and the company of other adoring men. She had been banished too long already to her friends on Earth and she hungered for social company and gaiety.

She bribed her blind guard with heavenly touches and kisses and escaped back to the women's court. All of the priestesses and hand women were happy to see her, and they disguised her as a hand maiden. She was able to attend all of the parties and orgies and her identity was not revealed because she kept a veil over her face which kept anyone from directly looking into her eyes.

Now, mythology tells that she found a baby named Adonis and raised him and eventually fell in love with him. That isn't how it happened. Adonis was created as an adult, an energy extension of Zeus and by Zeus alone, as a younger version of Zeus, but with a different personality, and with only the finer, high-minded parts woven in. And different ears! Adonis' ears were pointed. Adonis was to be a right-hand man, a totally loyal friend and companion who would be immortal and would stand beside Zeus and only Zeus for all time. Zeus wanted someone with joy and imagination to help him design and create creatures for Earth and other planets and dimensions. Zeus was the God of all, the Creator, and he was bored with his own ideas.

The gods and goddesses he created as an experiment in Olympus were mostly Diana's idea of a perfect world. Zeus became unhappy, and living with them was becoming a bore. Also, now, because of Aphrodite, jealousy and strife were causing problems in this perfect world. The gods wanted her and the goddesses hated her because she was more beautiful than they were.

Some of Zeus' creations worked and others didn't, so he was always busy creating things and destroying them as well. Everybody tried pretty hard around then not to make him mad, or 'ZAP.' Anyway, Zeus built Adonis to be oblivious to Aphrodite's charm, but he didn't count on Aphrodite falling in love with him.

Adonis was spending most of his time with Zeus. When Aphrodite saw him in the court at a celebration, she removed her veil and expected him to swoon over her like everyone else. He didn't. In fact he seemed repelled by her. She couldn't believe it. His rejection just enflamed her to have him, and her pursuit of him was merciless. He was bored with her shallow and immature efforts, for she thought that just being pretty was enough to get her anything. Adonis was more interested in studying and getting to be friends with intellectual people and interesting creatures who had something to share with him. Something to teach him.

Aphrodite set out to recreate herself into an interesting and stimulating companion and in the course of doing this, she found great satisfaction and joy in learning and becoming her own person again. She reconnected with the person who was wild in the woods of Earth and in the seas. She started to be moody and sullen and then became desperately lonely for what she had grown up with.

She lost interest in her child Aeneas, and she had long ago lost interest in Hephaestus and barely spent any time with them. She became depressed and ill and seemed to lose the will to live. Zeus and Diana watched their daughter deteriorate in despair. Nobody understood what was wrong. She was pining for what she could not have, and everyone believed, as she did, that it was for her old home, but Zeus was wiser than they were and thought he understood she wanted Adonis.

Zeus relented in an effort to save Aphrodite and planted a flame of passion for Aphrodite in Adonis, not so much to make him her slave, but enough to make it possible for them to be partners. Enough to make it possible for him to love her for herself. Zeus wished this change in Adonis, and it was done.

Because Zeus made Adonis a physician too, he called upon him to treat Aphrodite. Adonis showed such tender care that Aphrodite soon started to recover. They spent enough time together laughing and talking about everything that they soon realized they had become fast friends. That friendship grew to love.

Eventually Hephaestus found another love and released Aphrodite from her commitment to him. They still shared the child Aeneas, and Aphrodite eventually became a better mother to him.

Now Aphrodite was free, and she and Adonis became lovers. They produced a child, a beautiful little girl named Gwendolyn, with pointed ears like her father. Gwendolyn later became Queen of the Woodland Creatures and your ancestor.

Aphrodite loved Adonis, but still missed her Earth home too much. She soon became ill again and seemed to be dying. Adonis and Zeus and Diana didn't know what to do. She asked to be able to return home to Earth to die there. Because of the split-apart, only one could be in one dimension at a time. Zeus bent the 'rules' sufficiently to allow the dying Aphrodite to enter a portal to Earth at the exact time Persephone entered the sea portal to Olympus. He sent Adonis to Persephone to explain what was going on and to entreat her to exchange places and identities with Aphrodite. When Persephone saw Adonis, she fell in love with him, too, and so agreed to go to Olympus thinking she would be closer to him.

But Adonis stayed on Earth to take care of Aphrodite and their child who was to accompany her. They were all happy and free in their Garden of Eden, but she still sickened and died. She was the love of his life and even Zeus couldn't stop her from dying. Nobody at that time understood why she died, least of all the man called Spero now, who loved her more than anybody ever loved anyone.

His beautiful daughter Gwendolyn was all he had left of her, and in his final goodbye, he promised Aphrodite to always take care of their daughter and her family for the rest of time."

"And that includes you, Grandson." Spero put his hand on Peter's head.

He looked toward the door, "And you, granddaughter." Bette came around the corner, and she was crying. Spero hugged her and handed her a handkerchief,

"Blow." Bette blew a big loud honking blow.

"My dainty flower!" Spero and Peter laughed.

www.ingramcontent.com/pod-product-compliance
Lightning Source LLC
Chambersburg PA
CBHW070142100426
42743CB00013B/2795